Artificial Intelligence Using Ant Colony Optimization For Security Systems

Mubeen

TABLE OF CONTENTS

CHAPTER 1

INTRUSION DETECTION SYSTEM

This chapter highlights the increased risk of cyber threats, including viruses, worms, and hacker assaults, and addresses the expanding security difficulties that networks and devices face because of the growing number of connected devices. Network security has not been fully resolved despite a great deal of study into defense methods. This is mainly because attacker's computational resources are always evolving. The preparation, detection, and reaction phases of network security are described in this chapter, with an emphasis on Intrusion Detection Systems (IDS) [1], which are essential for spotting known and unexpected threats. The two primary detection methods anomaly and signature-based as well as the various IDS kinds, such as network and host-based systems, are covered. This chapter also examines IDS innovations, including hybrid technologies and cloud security, where specific difficulties, such as virtual machine threats and the issue of putting traditional security tools into practice, are addressed [2].

1.1 Background

Since the beginning, networked computers were seriously threatened by malware, Trojan horses, and assaults. In 2023, there were more Internet-connected gadgets than people on the planet, as seen in Figure 1.1, it is predicted that this growing trend would reach over seventy billion electronic devices till 2030. The security of these devices and the data that flow between them is a significant concern because of the rapid increase in invasions that occur each year. The previous research has looked at a variety of strategies for protecting against malicious attacks on networks in order to solve this problem [3]. Throughout twenty years of scientific investigation, the issue of network security has not been resolved. The quick development of invaders computing power and resources, which allows them to carry out intricate attacks, may be a reason for this. This can be thought of as a two-player game where the attacker must figure out the best way to stop the regular network operations, and the defense must choose the best defenses to prevent unintentional access to the networks or any computer system and make the information secure [4].

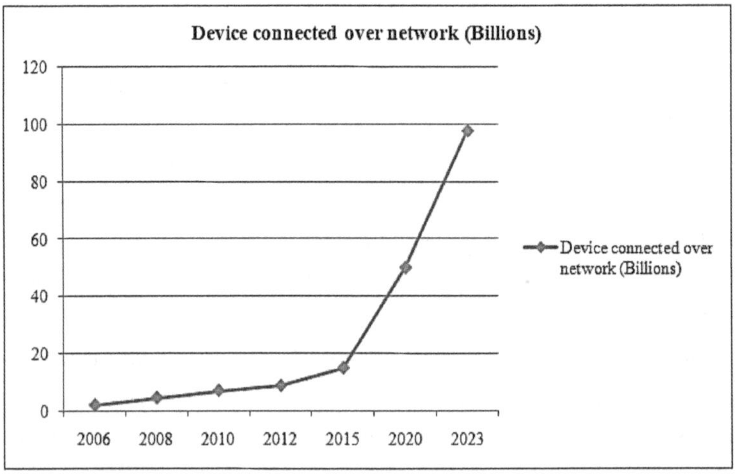

Figure 1.1: Growths of Internet-Connected Devices across Time [16]

Preparation, detection, and reaction phases are commonly included in network attack defense. To comprehend the situation and protect the assets, security engineers typically use a risk analysis approach throughout the all the phase. This process is crucial because it requires the technologists to comprehend how assaults occur as well as how they affect the computer system [5]. Depending on the information gathered, the preparation phase consists of identifying the vulnerabilities in the infrastructure, designing security measures, and deploying the required security equipment. Another essential component of network security is a detective system. To provide an effective cyber security solution, IDS typically works together with a firewall. "Detection is a must, but prevention is ideal" is one security principle. Being able to respond quickly requires the capacity to recognize assaults quickly. An automated detective stage is therefore quite important. Finally, during the reaction step, the intrusions found in a network are dealt with. A congestion obstructing technique is an illustration of a reduction technique applied during the reaction phase.

IDS are employed in conjunction with additional preventative safeguards like authorization and verification as a last resort to safeguard sensitive data resources. The defensive structure should incorporate IDS for a number of objectives. First, security was not considered when designing the traditional systems and applications. In other cases, programs and systems were developed to function in a variety of environments and are subject to risk when they are deployed. To improve system security, IDS works in tandem with defensive tactics [6]. Even in cases where preventive security measures are effective in protecting information systems, it is crucial to learn about intrusions that have occurred or are happening to understand security risks and dangers and to be prepared for future attacks. Several IDS prototypes were created starting with Denning's groundbreaking work in 1981.

IDS are a field of computer security that is still in its infancy because of the challenges in ensuring that information systems are free of security flaws. Instead, the hierarchy of security defects demonstrates that computer systems, regardless of their manufacturer, origin, or purpose, are vulnerable to security threats. Additionally, it is costly and technically complex, ensuring that computer networks and systems are secure from intrusions [7]. To perform a security status diagnostic on an information system, IDS collects data regarding the entire system. Finding any safety lapses, intended offenses, or weaknesses which may result in major violations constitutes the aim.

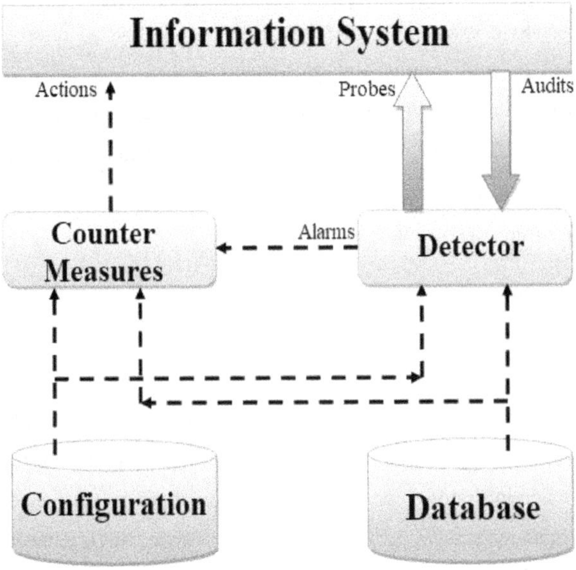

Figure 1.2: Basic Systems for Detecting Intrusions

Figure 1.2 illustrates the basic systems for detecting intrusions in which IDS comprises a detecting device that transforms data from a system into a very small, secure format. This detector could send audit probes that request application version numbers. It makes use of a variety of data: information pertaining to configuration about the current situation within the computer system, auditing information which describes what you've been occurring in the framework, and long-term information related to the technique for spotting intrusions (attacks knowledge base). The detector assists in eliminating unnecessary data from an audit trail, providing a compiled view of security-related activities conducted during routine system operation or a compiled view of the system's present security state [8]. The likelihood that these behaviors or states are indicators of intrusion or susceptibilities is determined. A countermeasure element guarantees mitigating action to prevent actions from being carried out or change the state of the system to one that is not protected. Information systems can better prepare for and manage threats with the help of IDS [9]. IDS collect data from various network and systems resources and analyses it to look for potential security issues. Intrusion detection is supported by:

- Tracking and evaluating system and user activity.
- System configuration and threat auditing.
- Assessing the accuracy of important data and system files.
- A statistical study of patterns of activity based on known assaults that match.
- Analysis of anomalous activities.
- Auditing the operating system.

1.2 IDS Components

IDS consists of following three components-

NIDS (Network Intrusion Detection System): It looks at all the traffic going through the subnet. It works in a promiscuous manner, matching subnet traffic to a library of named assaults. The administrator is notified as soon as an attack is discovered, or unusual activity is noticed. An admin can get the warning as soon as an assault is detected or unusual activity is noticed. It assists in cutting-edge cyber security threat response by strategically analyzing network activity utilizing signature-based techniques.

NNIDS (Network Node Intrusion Detection System): The internet transmission that goes to a specific host is examined by this mechanism. The fact that communication can only be tracked on an individual host instead of across the whole network is one way which NIDS as well as NNIDS vary from each other.

HIDS (Host based Intrusion Detection System): Each computer registry which is available is captured in the form of snapshot, which is then compared to a previous version. An alert is sent to an administration for the examination if any important system data are altered or deleted. The advent of the internet as a cellular network and the proliferation of connected devices have made it possible to obtain important information quickly, which has increased the number of replicated attacks due to the attacker's interest in this valuable information.

IDS are used to identify such activities that compromise the security and privacy of nearby computer systems. IDS come in two distinct forms: anomaly and signature-based. By examining received packet characteristics to a set of predetermined authentication, signature searches for known threats. Additionally, it must be updated frequently to ensure that there are enough; otherwise, recently known intrusions would go unnoticed because there would be no signature. Contrarily, IDS was developed to distinguish between normal and abnormal behavior, enabling more accurate identification of unidentified dangers. On the other side, it is expected that this detection method will generate a high number of false alarms: massive false positives could result in a real incursion being identified but disregarded through individuals, whereas systematic faults could give the appearance of security [10].

An inventive IDS was developed because of the increased sophistication of cyber threats that many businesses have had to deal with in recent years. Because every cyberattacks results in monetary losses, damage to one's reputation, and legal repercussions, the creation of IDS have universal effects for businesses as well as academia. Networks must be secured against unauthorized access, interaction with user and protection of data, and latest security vulnerabilities essentially made public. An effective security-enhancing tool for detecting and thwarting cyberattacks on any internet connection or host is the IDS [11]. IDSs are responsible for spotting questionable activity, making sure the network is sufficiently secure against intrusions, and reducing monetary and operational losses. IDS are the most effective tool for detection the abnormal activities.

IDSs can be classified as anomalous, signature, or a combination. The Signature-based IDS (SIDS), often referred to as standard IDS, continually watches internet activity and looks for patterns in incoming network data that match the signature of an assault. An attack's signature can be found by looking at the network packet headers, data sequences, and destination addresses of source network that fit for the malware model found, and packet series or data series linked to a particular attack. They are highly effective at detecting possible known intrusions because of their low failure rates. Since the administrator must manually update the system's dataset, SIDS can only identify interventions that are at present in the data record. Anomaly-based Intrusion Detection Systems (AIDS), examine the typical behavior of networks by regularly monitoring them for any indications of unusual activity. To identify novel kinds of intrusions, AIDS can either learn by utilizing anomaly detection techniques or educate it using reinforcement learning algorithms. When compared to signature-based systems, anomaly-based systems show variety in the identification of new threats [12][13].

Attackers find it difficult to define which infiltration actions will not be detected to alter any system's structural characteristics. Machine Learning-based AIDS (MLAIDS) improvement has recently been proposed. These algorithms identify the network status by classifying the information being processed into either typical or unusual categories. These methods undergo training and testing AIDS to assess AIDS capacities using various datasets. Despite this, a lot of datasets are not balanced. By combining the benefits of anomaly and signature systems, the hybrid IDS improves the detection of known intrusion threats. Deep learning techniques are used to shape the latest hybrid IDS. The advantages of AIDS in zero-day assaults lead to the presentation of the deeply learnt anomaly-based intrusion detection technique. IDS are an essential component of security since both known and undiscovered attacks are effectively detected. One of the main challenges in implementing these tactics is the large volume of activity that occurs during regular cloud operation, which makes it difficult to monitor and identify attacks. Soft computing's abilities to deal with both accurate and unclear information makes it ideal for identifying breaches. The hybrid classification methods are Support Vector Machine (SVM) and Artificial Neural Network (ANN) classification algorithms are applied in this work. It is employed to identify either normal or malicious activity [14][15].

Several common computing infrastructures and the general functioning of the computer systems are managed by a hypervisor inspector in a cloud environment. Because of its accessible nature and the amount of traffic it generates, hackers are finding the cloud to be more and more alluring. In particular, Distributed Denial of Service (DDoS) attacks are the second-most frequent cybercrime shortly after theft of identification. Flooding attacks using Transmission Control Protocol (TCP) and User Datagram Protocol (UDP), having the ability to swiftly exhaust the web's assets, consume the majority of its connectivity, and ruin every aspect of its operation. Because of such privacy dangers, an efficient intrusion system must be developed and put into place to protect the cloud against more frequent assaults, occasionally known as "zero-day breaches". Two of the most common issues with outdated methods are that IDS generate false alarms and fail to use sufficient criteria or criteria to assess risks. This may make the overuse issue worse [16][17].

1.3 Types of Intrusion Detection System

Network-IDS (NIDS) and another type of Host-IDS (HIDS) are the two primary categories of IDS. HIDS monitors the OS, whereas NIDS scans the internet traffic for unusual activities. A HIDS monitors system processes, important files, and applications on a single machine to spot any interior modifications performed by insiders. For notifying networking management of anomalous behavior, HIDS is commonly utilized. On the other hand, an NIDS operates at strategic points in networks to track cloud-based systems either internally and externally. It keeps an eye on every device linked to the network to spot any odd or malicious activity [18][19]. Each method has benefits and drawbacks of its own. Therefore, a combination of these methods can offer total cloud security. While NIDS keeps an eye out for external attacks on network-connected devices like routers, firewalls, print servers, switches and HIDS protects computers against internal threats. The effectiveness of an IDS is also determined by its configuration and intrusion detection techniques.

1.4 Functions of Intrusion Detection System

Numerous defensive mechanisms that can perform a range of tasks in a variety of environmental situations have been developed. The main element of a strong security system is an IDS [20], which correctly detects attacks before any action is taken. Finding the invasions prior to the network is seriously compromised is an IDS goal. An incursion is any illegal effort to gain entry to a network's resources in order to introduce vulnerabilities into the network's infrastructure. Figure 1.3 shows an extended IDS design which start with data collection, data processing and with the help on intrusion model we detect the attacks and generate the alarm.

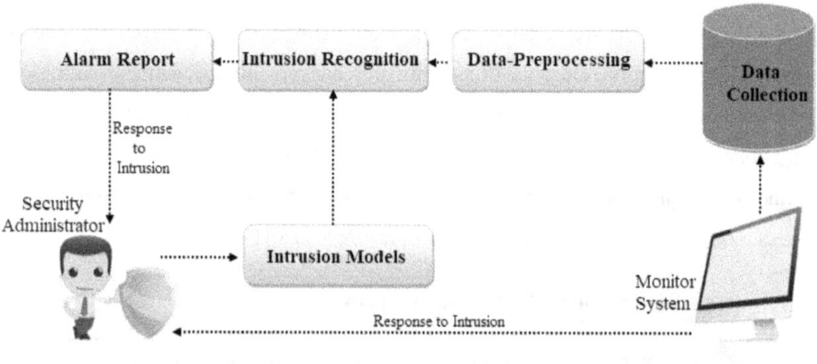

Figure 1.3: Extended Intrusion Detection Systems

The two main categories of IDS are anomaly along with signature-based. Signature-based IDSs categorize interactions with the network using an established library or widely recognized endorsements, whereas anomaly-based IDSs generate an average customer profiles and mark whatever corresponds to that description as a malicious attempt. Consequently, the majority of businesses incorporate a great deal of such an approach. The recognition of unknown incursions is one of the main problems with signature-based intrusion detection. The online dataset's of rules has to be updated manually or automatically on a regular basis in order to address this issue. An automatic procedure can be carried out using supervised learning techniques, whereas a manual process usually gets carried out by a system administrator who obtains fresh signatures and adds those to the dataset's of rules. Using an anomaly detection framework, that can recognize novel attack types, is another way to address this issue [23][24]. However, distinguishing between typical and unusual behavior is the main difficulty encountered by anomaly detection systems. Additionally, a system for detecting anomalies needs to adapt to the changing nature of the general traffic pattern, which changes over time. Presently, both approaches must be flexible due to the quick development of innovation and the expanding range of techniques for hacking accessible. To be able to respond to network breaches as quickly as feasible, an IT-driven or a minimum semi-automated monitoring component is necessary. Because a system for early detection allows for more time to react appropriately, this will lesser the amount of harm done to authorized users [21][22].

1.5 Cloud Computing Based IDS

There are further problems with the cloud computing three services model that need to be resolved to secure the user model. Infrastructure as a Service (IaaS) can be impacted, for instance, by attacks like hijacking of the Domain Name System, IP tampering hypervisor flaws, remote computer invasions and information thefts. According to studies, Platform as a Service (PaaS) might be the subject of phishing, which Man-in-the-Middle assaults including inspection of ports, whereas Software as a Service (SaaS) is susceptible to Denial-of-Service (DoS) harm, identification risks, and SQL injection flaws. As a result, a structure which can safeguard itself from threats and illicit activities is required. To provide cloud security, cloud computing based IDS have been developed [24].

1.5.1 Necessity of Cloud Security

Since cloud-based services have been offered to customers online, there are greater security risks for both the user and the cloud provider. The ones that follow represent a few elements that impact cloud system safety and confidentiality:

The primary component of safety in the cloud involves the fact that customer applications and information are kept on the supplier's property. Web hosting companies forbid consumers from using their safety alternatives, which reach beyond the administrative section, due to worries about confidentiality. Additionally, the cloud is built on virtualization, which allows clients to share resources, increasing the risk of privacy problems and making security model development more difficult.

Attacks provide the biggest security threat to cloud providers. These may originate from either the subscriber or the supplier. Consequently, a system that can offer defense against malevolent actions is required to protect our data from the unauthorized access.

1.5.2 Current Cloud Computing IDS

Several intrusion detection methods are categorized and examined in this section. The IDS strategies used in this work have been divided into five groups according to their setup, positioning, and the types of assaults they are able to identify as seen in Figure 1.4.

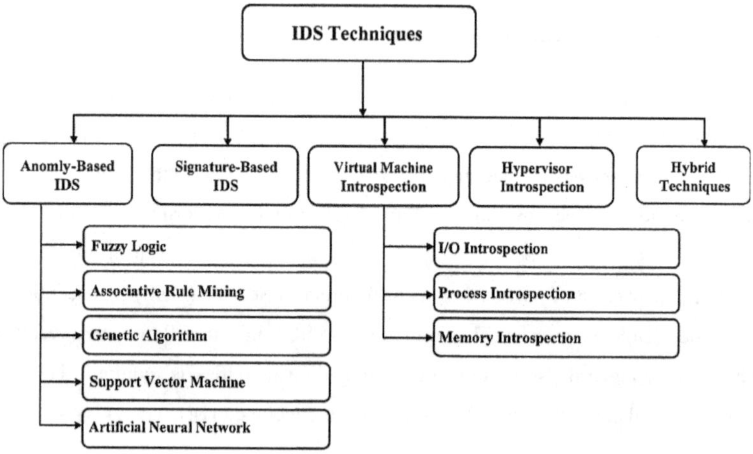

Figure 1.4: Cloud IDS Techniques Classification [24]

1.5.2.1 Anomaly Detection-based IDS

Although it detects recognized attacks quickly and has relatively small false positive rates, Regular signature updating of dataset's is required for IDS that relies on signatures. To overcome the limitations of signature-based IDS, approaches for detecting abnormalities are being designed. By examining user activity, this technique creates a behavioral profile. Then, known and new assaults are identified using this behavioral profile. The fundamental structure of an anomaly detection technique is shown in Figure 1.5. The learning process as well as the identification phases is its two primary stages. The characteristic generating component collects and analyzes information obtained from the underlying system or network in order to produce features throughout the training portion of the process. The training component uses these traits in order to create a behavioral framework. The data is divided into two categories using this method: typically occurring actions and abnormal conduct. In the anomaly detection stage, intruders are found using this model. An alarm is sent to the network manager for any deviation from regular traffic, which is deemed an intrusion. This approach may recognize novel attacks, but it requires additional computing resources. The security manager is now responsible for determining the cause of the alarm, which is generated by any departure from regular behavior [27].

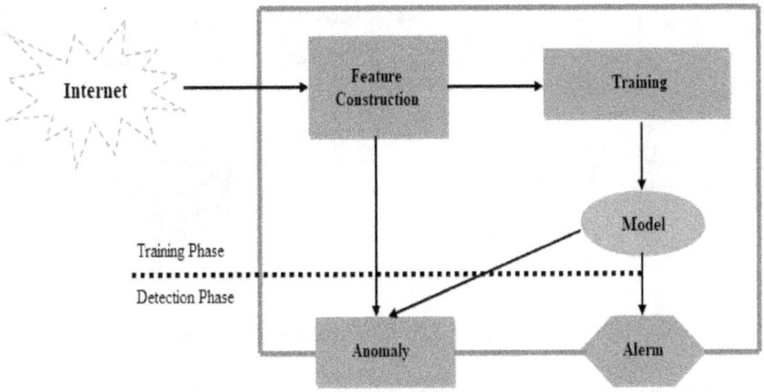

Figure 1.5: Models for Detecting Anomalies

1.5.2.2 Signature based IDS

By contrasting it with established trends or harmful directions, signatures intrusion detection systems are able to identify anomalous activity. It maintains a signature-based registry that monitors a multitude of threats and malicious activities. It is necessary to continually update that signature library in order to identify emerging risks. To find any malicious behavior, the present-day network transmissions undergo comparison to the stored set of criteria. Another of the simplest and most widely used signature-based methods is Snort. The well-known IDS that is signature-based is used for capturing packets and real-time web traffic monitoring. Its main parts the pre-processor, packet decoding, logging, discovery engine, and warning scheme that are shown in Figure 1.6. The present-day internet traffic is pre-processed before it reaches the detecting mechanism. Throughout this phase, unnecessary or unfinished information is removed. The scanning machine subsequently compares the freshly obtained traffic against the items in the signing dataset's. If an association turns up, a notification is sent to the relevant managers; if not, the data packet is transmitted as usual. To identify recognized attacks in a cloud context, numerous academics have proposed signature-based IDS, like a rule-based NIDS [25]. Information from each virtual machine's operating system is gathered and updated dynamically for configuring the detection rules [26].

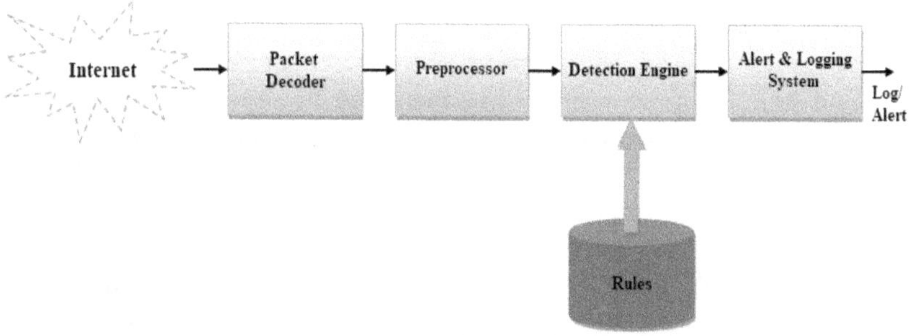

Figure 1.6: IDS based on Signatures

1.5.2.3 IDS based on Virtual Machine Introspection (VMI)

The strategic positioning of IDS is essential to the attack monitoring approach. IDS provide a thorough overview of network activity once installed on a host, but it is vulnerable to assaults. IDS installed in a cloud-based setting, on the other hand, are less vulnerable to attacks but provides less systems transparency. Similarly, doing research using the tenant's virtual computer may expose it to advanced threats like malware. Additionally, the monitored virtual machine security is easily breached. Consequently, a technique that divides IDS from the currently observed virtual machine is required. Using a safety precaution in Virtual Machine Manager (VMM) is one way to do this is involved. The intrusion identification approach known as Virtual Machine Introspection, or VMI, collects data at the hypervisor layers to keep an eye on Virtual Machine (VM) via the outside. Figure 1.7 illustrates the fundamental framework of the VMI approach, in which the monitoring virtual machine uses a Lib VMI package to obtain information concerning state regarding the virtual machine under observation. To decode whatever is contained in VM using the initial information, the Lib VMI packaging the fundamental part that comprises the VMI technique is utilized. To collect information from observed virtual machines, researchers use a range of methods, involving as Input/output (I/O) introspection, processing introspection, system activity, and memory introspection. Methods based on memory introspection collect information from main memory.

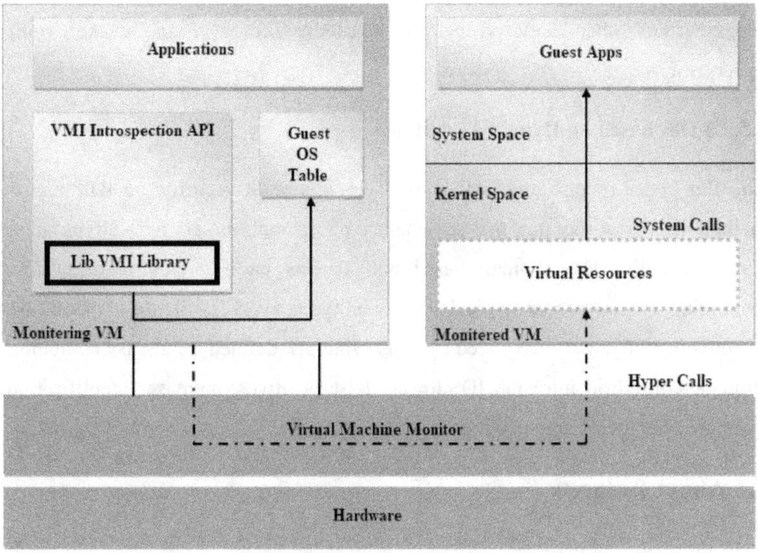

Figure 1.7: Introspection of Virtual Machines

1.5.2.4 IDS based on Hypervisor-Introspection (HVI)

Dynamical program assessment requires the monitoring instrument to be in a running state, A hacker may still breach the system being watched even when the person who is monitoring employing VMI methods is far away from it. Furthermore, the hypervisor must be an encrypted platform to allow the VMI software to work in order for the VMI technique to work. However, a National Institute of Standards and Technology (NIST) study found that the Xen and VMware ESX hypervisors are equally susceptible to intrusions [25]. Virtual Machines can be targeted if the hypervisor is hacked. As a result, Hypervisor Introspection (HVI), a revolutionary method, has been presented, which applies safety measures under the hypervisor level instead of at the hypervisor. This approach examines the memory of the hypervisor, data structures, hyper calls, control, and non-control stream data. For example, a protection model is set up beneath the Virtual Machine Monitor (VMM) in layered hypervisor security architecture. The underlying premise of this paradigm is that data within visitor virtual machines is unaffected by errors in the VMM. The Hyper Lock technique, which operates a virtual machine in a different address space, is similar. This analysis suggests that other cloud virtual machines are secure if an attacker compromises a hypervisor.

1.5.2.5 IDS based on Hybrid Techniques

To offer better precise and dependable surveillance of security, an IDS built on a hybrid methodology incorporates the advantages of anomaly-based as well as signature-based detection tools. The anomaly-based half detects undiscovered or zero-day threats by examining anomalies from typical activity on the network, while the signature-based section effectively recognizes recognized assaults using pre-defined trends. By combining these two strategies, a hybrid intrusion IDS lowers false positives, increases identification precision, and boosts resilience to changing online threats.

1.6 About Datasets

In below section lots of dataset based on Intrusion detection model is discussed along with their details but the major concert related to all available dataset is data preprocessing. For these lots of approaches like replacing null values, feature scaling, feature aggregation, and dimensionality reduction are required for cleaning the dataset [12].

1.6.1 KDD Dataset

KDD stands for Knowledge Discovery in Dataset. Finding information and crucial trends in massive volumes of information is the aim of this multifaceted field. To find important insights and make wise judgments, KDD integrates methods from a variety of domains, including statistics, data mining, machine learning, and dataset's systems.

There are usually multiple steps in the KDD process:

1. Data Cleaning: To deal with noise, missing values, and inconsistencies, the raw data must be preprocessed and cleaned in this step.

2. Information Integration: In this process, data across several different sources is combined jointly to create one large set of data for evaluation.

3. Data Selection: Based on predetermined standards and goals, pertinent subsets of data are chosen for examination.

4. Data Transformation: The chosen data is changed into formats that are suitable for mining. This could entail preprocessing methods like normalization, aggregation, or discretization.

5. The KDD process is data mining, when a variety of algorithms and methods are used to glean patterns, correlations, relationships, and other intriguing information from the data.

6. Evaluation of the Patterns: The identified patterns are assessed considering predetermined standards, such as novelty, utility, validity, or interest.

7. Knowledge Presentation: The last phase is analyzing and providing users with a relevant and intelligible presentation of the knowledge that has been mined. Effective communication can be achieved using interactive tools, reporting, or visualization approaches.

8. Predictive modeling: KDD will be used to create models that predict patterns and trends in the future.

Healthcare, marketing, business, finance, and the social sciences are just a few of the fields in which KDD finds extensive use. It helps businesses to learn from their data, spot patterns, forecast outcomes, make better decisions, and uncover important information that can boost productivity, effectiveness, and competitiveness [12]. The KDD primary benefit is that it enhances decision-making. KDD offers useful information and insights that can improve decision-making and boost productivity for businesses. KDD saves both money and time and improves customer service by automating time-consuming and repetitive operations and preparing the data for analysis. Organizations can improve customer service by better understanding the wants and preferences of their customers with the use of KDD. Fraud detection: By spotting trends and irregularities in data that can point to fraud, KDD may be employed to find fraudulent activity, such as identifying abnormal patterns and suspicious behaviors in large-scale transactional and network data to support proactive security.

1.6.2 KDD Cup 99

The KDD Cup 99 dataset is a popular source of data. In the discipline related to network intrusion detection. By mimicking network traffic, this dataset simulates an intrusion detection situation on a Local Area Network (LAN). It comprises a vast amount of data about network traffic that has been collected from both routine activities and a range of attack scenarios. The competition's objective was to create IDS's that could differentiate between malicious and legitimate network traffic. Because of its age, the KDD Cup 1999 dataset is not anymore, a particularly current or relevant dataset for assessing IDS's. It is still often used, nevertheless, for testing, comparison, and research. It offers a historical viewpoint and helps comprehend the difficulties encountered in the early stages of wireless intrusion detection [12].

1.6.3 NSL_KDD

A standard datasets which is extensively utilized in the domains of surveillance of networks as well as online safety is the Network Security Laboratory-KDD Cup 1999, or NSL_KDD [14]. The dataset available from the NSL_KDD was created to address a few issues with the original KDD Cup 1999 dataset, such as the presence of superfluous and repetitive elements. It is meant to replicate a more rigorous and authentic environment for assessing malware detection systems. Congestion on networks data collected from a computer simulation makes up the NSL_KDD dataset. It includes both typical network traffic and several kinds of attacks; this covers techniques such as Remote-to-Local (R2L) assault, Denial-of-Service (DoS) attack, User-to-Root (U2R), and probing. The labeled dataset classifies each item either according to normal or as a member of one of the targeted categories. In addition to a variety of mathematical variables extracted from TCP/IP headers, the dataset generated by the NSL-KDD includes network link attributes including service, protocol type, destination, origin IP addresses, starting point, and final destination. These ports Academic as well as business specialists regularly employ the dataset provided by Network Security Laboratory (NSL) in order to generate and assess strategies for safeguarding network connections and IDS's. It offers a commonly accepted and standardized criterion by which to compare various network security methodologies. Although the dataset created by NSL_KDD has been used extensively in the recent past, it has several drawbacks, such as a several possibilities for attacks and the potential for it to not accurately capture the intricacies and features of actual network traffic.

1.6.4 CIC-IDS2017

CIC-IDS2017 an evaluation dataset for intrusion detection, IDS and Intrusion Prevention Systems (IPSs) are extremely important defences toward the increasing complexity and frequency of computer network assaults. Improving anomaly-based IDS accuracy and dependability has been hampered by the absence of dependable evaluation and verification datasets. The majority of the eleven statistics we examined, which have been published since 1998, are out dated and untrustworthy.

A few dataset's do not offer sufficient data heterogeneity and quantity, whereas other dataset's fail to include the range of identified dangers, even if many disguise packet payloads knowledge, making it hard to record present patterns. Additionally, some dataset's lack sets of features and metadata. The dataset generated by CIC-IDS2017 contains both normal traffic and the most recent, well-known assaults, and it closely mimics genuine actual-world information. It includes the outcomes of network usage evaluation carried out together with labeled flows that include timestamps, the starting and ending IP addresses, beginning and intended ports, and methods. The definition of the retrieved features is also accessible. When creating this dataset, the main goal was to provide realistic background traffic. Heart bleed, DoS, Infiltration, Web Attack, Botnet, DDoS, Brute Force FTP, Brute Force SSH, and others are among the attacks [28]. The CIC-IDS2017 dataset's salient characteristics include:

Network Traffic: Network traffic recordings from an actual business network environment are included in the collection. It covers legitimate and malicious traffic as well as a broad spectrum of threats from hackers, such as botnet processes, Distributed Denial-of-Service (DDoS) assaults, port scans as well and more.

Attack Scenarios: The dataset's includes a range of attack scenarios, such as exploitation attempts, Control and Command (C&C) communications, network reconnaissance, and malware of various kinds. The purpose of these scenarios is to simulate actual cyber threats and attack trends.

Labeling and Ground Truth: Labeled examples of whether a network flow is an attack or a typical activity are provided by the CIC-IDS2017 dataset. Supervised learning and assessment of IDS methods and algorithms are made possible by this ground truth labeling.

Traffic properties: The dataset contains a wide range of properties that were taken from the network traffic, including transport-layer characteristics, flow statistics, and packet attributes. These characteristics can be entered into a machine. By using these properties of the dataset researchers can filter the dataset very well.

Researchers, security experts, and developers can evaluate the efficacy of their detection and prevention strategies, contrast various IDS systems, and progress around cyber security due to the CIC-IDS2017 dataset. It supports the creation of trustworthy and precise IDS's and encourages standardization and repeatability in the evaluation of IDS solutions.

1.7 Machine Learning Techniques

The goal of Machine Learning (ML) is to create computations and algorithms that let computers comprehend and predict or execute choices without explicitly coding. It entails the development and analysis of systems that are capable of automatically learning from data or experience [2]. Machines to recognize patterns, draw conclusions, and anticipate or react to input requiring specific programming is the fundamental concept of machine learning. Algorithmic models for ML can take many different shapes, such as-

1.7.1 Supervised Learning

Labeled information is used for teaching the algorithm in controlled learning, wherein the information being provided matches predetermined goal indicates or outcomes. In order to determine how to link the information being supplied with the appropriate output, the method looks for connections and patterns in the labeled instances. Neural networks, Support Vector Machines (SVM) [5], and decision trees are commonly used methods for supervised learning. Supervised learning is a machine learning approach in which models are trained using labeled data to learn the mapping between input features and known output classes for accurate prediction, commonly used for classification and regression tasks, and it relies on annotated datasets to evaluate and improve model performance.

1.7.2 Unsupervised Learning

Unsupervised learning involves the use of unlabeled information, in which goal labels or objectives are not provided. Finding sequences, frameworks, or relationships in the data is the aim. Principal Component Analysis (PCA) and grouping approaches are examples of dimensionality-reducing strategies used in unsupervised training.

1.7.3 Reinforcement Learning

During experimentation to positive reinforcement, an agent learns to interact using its surroundings and choose the best course of conduct. The agent is guided to make better decisions over time via feedback or rewards that are given based on its activities. In fields including autonomous systems, gaming, and robotics, reinforcement learning is frequently employed.

1.7.4 Semi-Supervised Learning

Unsupervised and supervised educational components are combined in semi-supervised instruction. Techniques are trained through the mixture of with labels and unlabeled information while unlabeled information being utilized to enhance training.

A machine learning algorithm is a set of guidelines or processes that, ignoring the need for explicit code, allow machines to acquire knowledge from facts and make judgments or judgments. The algorithms used here identify similarities in data rather than obeying predetermined instructions, which enables them to get better with time.

- **K-Nearest Neighbour (KNN)**

One simple method is K-Nearest Neighbour [21]. The KNN algorithm places new data into the group that appears most related to the existing categories based on the assumption that additional information and current cases are comparable. The algorithm known as KNN can categorize incoming data points according to how similar they are to the known dataset by storing all the relevant data. This makes it simple to use the KNN algorithm to classify new data into appropriate groups. The KNN algorithm is mostly used for classification problems, even though it may be used for regression as well. KNN does not depend on any presumptions regarding the underlying data because it is not a quantitative approach. Instead of immediately understanding form the source data set, it keeps the information and performs operations to it throughout categorization; it is frequently referred to by the term a lazy learner algorithm. When new data is discovered within the training phase, the algorithm known as KNN merely accumulates the dataset and categorizes it according to an arrangement that closely matches the new data. For example, a picture that looks like both a dog and a cat, and you must decide if it's a dog or a cat. The KNN method can be applied in this situation by utilizing similarity metrics with regard to the majority of similar characteristics, the model trained on KNN will categorize the newly collected data into the relevant cat or dog group while evaluating its qualities by contrasting it with previously taken images of dogs and cats. [32].

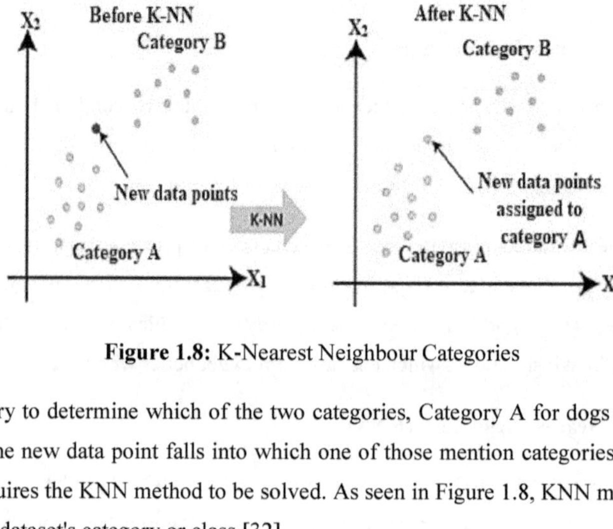

Figure 1.8: K-Nearest Neighbour Categories

It is necessary to determine which of the two categories, Category A for dogs and Category B for cats, the new data point falls into which one of those mention categories. This kind of problem requires the KNN method to be solved. As seen in Figure 1.8, KNN makes it simple to identify a dataset's category or class [32].

The method that follows explains how KNN functions: Initially an indicator for K, which represents the entire number of adjacent neighbors, is chosen; next, the Euclidean distance to the K adjacent neighbors is calculated; and lastly, the number of knowledge places within every group is measured. When our algorithm is at last complete and the number of neighbors is at its maximum, we then allocate the extra data values to that category.

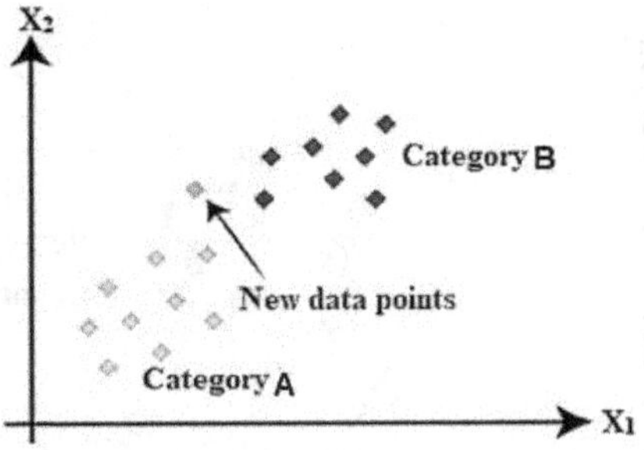

Figure 1.9: KNN New Data Point [21]

Figure 1.9 will be used to illustrate new Data Point. The Euclidean distance among the data points must be computed after the number of neighbors has been determined. The distance that exists between two points, as depicted in Figure 1.10, is the Euclidean distance. It can be computed using below formula as mention in equation 1.1.

Euclidean Distance of A and B = $\sqrt{((X_2 - X_1)^2 + (Y_2 - Y_1)^2)}$................(1.1)

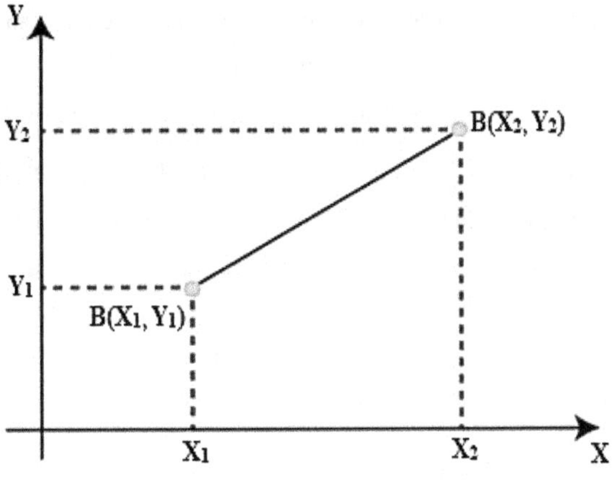

Figure 1.10: Distance Curvature

The closest neighbors are determined by computing the Euclidean distance; as seen in Figure 1.11, categories A and B have three and two nearest neighbors, respectively.

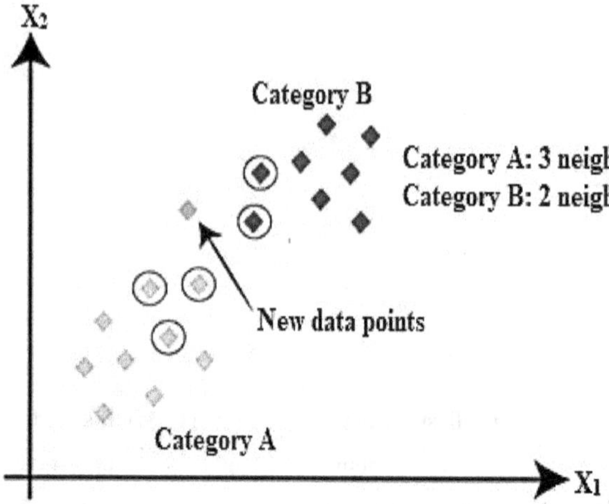

Figure 1.11: Choosing the Neighboring Points

That new data point needs to be placed under category A since the three closest neighbors are clearly from that category. Therefore, there is no specific method for figuring out the ideal value for K. Five is the most favored value for K. Extremely low values for K, like K=1 or K=2, might cause noise and result in the model's outlier effects.

Easy execution, resilience to polluted data used for training, and the possibility of greater efficacy with bigger training sets of information are some advantages of the KNN. KNN drawbacks include the necessity to constantly calculate the value of K, which can occasionally be difficult, and the high computing cost resulting from figuring out the distance between each training sample's data points. Thus, the SVM and ANN hybrid algorithms are applied for this research.

- **Algorithm for Support Vector Machines**

Encouragement Issues relating to regression and classification may be solved with algorithms for supervised learning called vector machines, or SVM for short. However, its primary use is in categorizing problems. Creating a line of decision or hyper-axis that may divide the information into discrete groups is the primary objective of SVM [32].

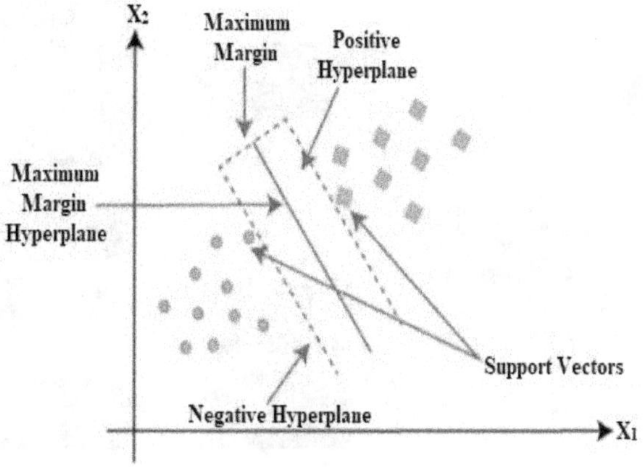

Figure 1.12: Support Vector Machine

These support vectors, or the information pieces that help define the hyper plane, are what give the method employed in support vector machines their name as shown in Figure 1.12, SVM has several practical uses, including drug discovery, picture classification, and face detection.

- **Deep Learning**

A subfield of ML are called Deep Learning (DL) focuses on multi-layered neural networks, sometimes referred to as deep neural networks. Models based on DL may provide extremely expressive and effective algorithms for voice and visual recognition purposes by automatically acquiring data with hierarchical structures [29]. The manner in which robots comprehend, acquire knowledge and engage with complicated material is being revolutionized by DL. By simulating the neural networks seen in the human brain, DL allows systems to automatically find sequences and draw well-informed conclusions.

Structures that effortlessly uncover undetected trends in facts, predict outcomes, and boost efficacy according to previous results. Multiple strategies can be applied to various problems in ML. For instance, the KNN technique is effective for classification issues, whereas conventional linear regression may be employed for predictive scenarios such as forecasting patterns of trading. Figure 1.13 shows the classifications of ML techniques.

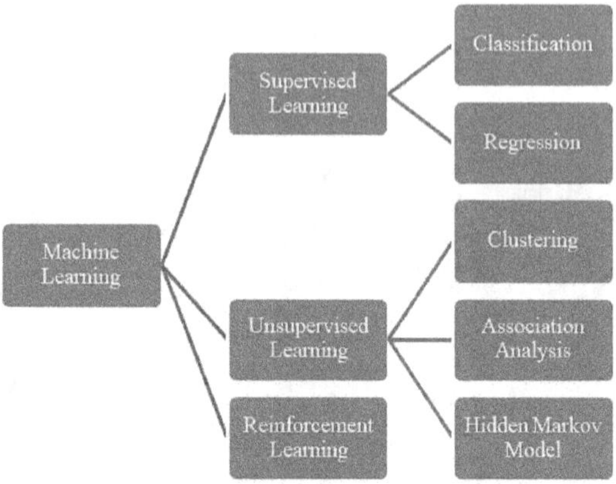

Figure 1.13: Classifications of ML Techniques

1.8 Clustering

The process of clustering involves breaking up unlabelled data points or data into distinct groups so that comparable data points are grouped together and those that are different from one another are grouped together. To put it simply, clustering is the process of separating groups that share traits and organizing them into groups or clusters. There are two broad categories into which clustering can be divided:

a. Hard Computing: All the input data points in hard clustering are either totally or partially part of a cluster. For example, every data set belongs to one of the various groupings.
b. Soft Clustering: With soft clustering, each input data point is given a probability of being in those clusters. Rather than placing every point of data into a distinct cluster. For instance, each piece of data is given a likelihood of falling into one of the dataset's many clusters.

1.8.1 Clustering Algorithms

The researchers studied a larger variety of clustering algorithms, however just a few of the algorithms covered below are widely employed [30].

1.8.1.1 Models of Connectivity

The premise behind these ideas is that information points in a statistical area which are near one another appear to be similar to those which were separated by a distance. These representations are applicable to two different methods. In the first method, all of the data points are first divided into distinct clusters, which are subsequently combined when the space within them gets less. Once all of the data elements have been properly categorized as a single cluster, a second approach divides them as the distance grows. Furthermore, there is flexibility in selecting the distance function. These models are simple to understand, but they aren't scalable enough to handle big datasets. These kinds of structures include organizational clustering techniques and their varying forms.

1.8.1.2 Centroids

These iterative clustering techniques use the proximity of data points to group centroids in order to determine similarity. One popular example of a technique that falls into this group is the K-Means clustered approach. It is crucial to comprehend the dataset beforehand for these models as they demand previous knowledge of the total number of clusters.

These algorithms operate iteratively to determine the optimal location. On the basis of it chose the new data points.

1.8.1.3 Models of Distribution

Such types of clustering are based on the probability that every statistic in the group belongs to the same distribution, such as Normal or Stochastic. Over-fitting is a prevalent problem with these models. The Expectation-maximization strategy, which makes utilization of multidimensional standard distributions, is a renowned illustration of such ideas.

1.8.1.4 Models of Density

These mathematical frameworks look for regions in the data field where the information point concentration varies. Following the isolation of different dense zones, data points within these parts are allocated to comparable groupings. Density-based Spatial Clustering of Applications with Noise (DBSCAN) and ordering points. To identify the clustering structure OPTICS are well-known models for density-based clustering. These models are highly useful for identifying outliers and clusters of whatever form since they are able to discriminate between points that are located in dense and sparse regions of the data space.

1.8.2 K-Means Algorithm

K-Means methods have more advantages than the other algorithms in the four models mentioned.

a. K-Means clustering's linear time complexity allows it to handle large data sets effectively.
b. Because the clusters are chosen at random, the K-Means clustering results obtained by repeating the procedure may vary.
c. It is discovered that K-Means performs best when the clusters have a hyper spherical shape, such as a sphere in 3D or a circle in 2D.

K-Means Clustering Algorithm:

Finding local maxima in each iteration is the goal of the iterative clustering algorithm K-Means. The objective is to divide n data points into k clusters, where every finding is a member of the clusters containing the closest mean. There are five steps of algorithm:

Step 1: Indicate how many clusters (K).

Step 2: Every statistic is assigned to a clusters at arbitrary.

Step 3: Determine the centroids of the clusters

Step 4: Each individual point should be assigned to the nearest cluster center.

Step 5: Recalculate each cluster's centroids.

When no improvements are possible, repeat steps 4 and step 5: The fourth and fifth phases will be repeated in a similar manner until we achieve the global optima, which are reached after two consecutive repetitions in which no data points are switched between the two clusters. If not specifically stated, it will indicate that the algorithm has ended.

This K indicates that the clustering algorithm is quick and reasonably effective. The result is computed at $O(tK_n)$ when n is the total amount of locations or objects where t is the repetition interval and K is the number of groupings. At local optimum, it frequently comes to an end. The global optimum can be found using methods like genetic algorithms or simulated annealing. However, when there are fewer data points, the cluster will be mostly determined by the initial grouping. This necessitates prior knowledge of the amount of groupings, K. Its drawback is of not always yielding the same result since the final clusters depend on the initial random assignments.

Since a different order of input could result in a different cluster if there are few data points, the actual cluster remains unknown using the same data. It is susceptible to the starting state. Cluster results can vary depending on the original conditions. It's possible that the algorithm is stuck at the local optimum. The K-Means method is comparatively easy to use and helpful for undirected knowledge discovery. Artificial intelligence, machine vision, pattern recognition, image processing, classification analysis, unsupervised neural network learning, and many more domains have found widespread use for K-Means.

1.9 Feature Selection Techniques

A technique called extraction of features was created to simplify the information in order to increase the method's mistake detection capabilities and reduce the False Alarm Rate (FAR). Given the quantity of computer networks expanded, so did the amount, variety, and speed of information from several sources. The information has to be processed and stored for subsequent use. But the efficacy of the structure can deteriorate if this information is delivered straight into the IDS component. Fundamental audit data of online traffic doesn't seem suitable for malware detection while not all the properties are helpful in identifying an incursion. There are 41 qualities in each network packet, which yield 241-1 subsets in total. In addition to being challenging to manage, the cost and memory usage are increased by the massive number of subgroups. Internet connection attributes are further classified into three groups based on their importance for assault identification: moderately pertinent extremely pertinent, and inconsequential.

To increase the accuracy and efficacy of the framework, it is crucial to simplify and eliminate unnecessary characteristics from the very first analysis of the initial collection of information. Feature selection, which seeks to preserve the features that most accurately reflect the original data, is one way to do this. This method retains the characteristics that best represent the primary data while eliminating extraneous elements. However, as the accuracy of the system depends on the particular characteristics used for intrusion detection, proper implementation is essential. Several academics have been creating different feature selection methods, such as a Genetic Algorithm (GA) based strategy. They argue that choosing the right collection of characteristics is a difficult and drawn-out process that could need the supervision of subject matter specialists.

1.9.1 Classification of Data

Since each audit record can be allocated to a different set of potential categories, such as typical behavior or a particular form of intrusion, the idea of intrusion detection can be thought of as a categorization puzzle. The use of cloud-based intrusion detection has grown in popularity in recent years. They developed models for both abuse and anomaly identification based on observed behaviors in the audit data by applying several methodologies.

Bayesian Classification, Decision Trees, Neural Networks, Associative Classification, SVM, k-Nearest Neighbor Classifiers, and Rule Induction Methods are among the classification techniques frequently used for intrusion detection datasets. Applying common algorithms to publicly accessible intrusion detection datasets is the foundation of many of these strategies. However, when computer incursions are far less often than typical behavior, ordinary categorization methods sometimes perform badly.

In these situations, researchers have created specialized algorithms designed to address intrusion detection issues. Additionally, improving the classification accuracy of current methods and algorithms is still a difficult undertaking, especially when it comes to identifying novel attack types. Overcoming these obstacles and creating reliable classifiers are prerequisites for constructing effective IDS.

1.9.2 Methods of Optimization Using Genetic Algorithms

An effective strategy for determining the ideal balance between the given design characteristics and operational circumstances is optimization. This procedure lowers the risks and expenses related to operation and design while directing the experimental efforts. Optimizing is a method of determining the ranges for decision factors that result in the lowest or greatest consequences of particular aims. The function objectives description and the optimization strategy are used to assess the best solutions' dependability. Optimizing a process requires an analytical structure that can describe and predict its behavior. Optimizing screening may be useful for estimating unanticipated variables in intricate systems that are not linear. Robust optimization may be able to detect uncertain variables in processes that are dynamic. Multiphase reactor and flow system design and scale-up approach could be made possible using optimization as a tool.

A genetic algorithm is an analysis and improvement method that utilizes the concepts of selection by chance and biology. By simulating the evaluation process, it is utilized to solve complicated problems. A genetic algorithm's fundamental concept is to generate a population of those that could be used to solve a problem. Everyone has been encoded as a collection of factors, commonly referred to as a genotype or chromosome, which can be combined and altered to create new individuals. Depending on the issue area, these parameters can alternatively be encoded as real numbers or data structures; however they are usually represented as binary strings. Complex searching and optimization difficulties, particularly non-linear ones or ones, can be successfully solved by genetic algorithms.

A method that combines the concepts of the genetic approach with Particle Swarm Optimization (PSO) [31], to tackle optimization issues is called a hybrid algorithm. The goal of this hybrid strategy is to take advantage of both GA exploration and PSO exploitation capabilities. Like a conventional GA, the hybrid algorithm represents the GA population's members as chromosomes. A possible solution to the issue being optimized is encoded by each chromosome. To find the optimal solution, the PSO component adds a particles swarm that travel through the solution space.

The combined approach can effectively investigate the solution space, look for superior solutions, and convergence towards optimal or nearly optimal solutions by fusing the exploration and exploitation capabilities of GA and PSO. It's crucial to remember that the hybrid method's exact details regarding implementation and value of parameters might vary depending on the requirements of the program and the issue being solved. The hybrid techniques performance depends on how well the PSO and GA components are integrated and modified for this specific issue domain [32].

The Beetle Swarming Process is then used in the improvement phase; each insect represents a potential solution for the optimal issue, and each bug is equal to a fitness value determined by the function called fitness. Similar to the particle swarm approach, the beetles communicate data, but their distance and direction are controlled by their rate of motion and the intensity of their data that the long antennas can detect. This BSO algorithm performs more consistently. When the beetle search method is incorporated into the optimization process, the algorithm performs better globally and converges more quickly. The BSO algorithm can answer more difficult problems and can strike a balance between an individual's exploration and exploitation. BSO is therefore also used here.

Then, the Oppositional Crow Search Approach (OCSA) represents a Meta heuristic optimization method that draws inspiration from opposition-based learning and crow foraging behavior. To improve the Crow Search Algorithms (CSA) capacity for exploration and exploitation, it was suggested as an addition. A population of crows in OCSA is a representation of possible solutions to an optimization issue. Every crow represents a potential solution and has a corresponding fitness value that shows how good it is. By relocating the crows according to their fitness and interactions with one another, the program seeks to iteratively enhance the population. Opposition-based learning, which entails developing opposing solutions throughout the optimization process, is the fundamental concept underlying OCSA. The opposing answer for every crow is produced by reflecting its location in relation to a specific reference point. The method seeks to explore various areas of searching space and increase convergence speed by considering simultaneously the original and opposing solutions. Numerous optimization issues, such as function optimization, parameter tuning, and feature selection have been addressed by the OCSA.

1.10 Artificial Neural Networks

Giving machines human-like comprehension and decision-making capabilities, the goal of Artificial Neural Networks (ANN) is to mimic the neural structure that makes up the brain of a person. Artificial neural networks are made by programming computers to behave like linked brain cells. There are around 1000 billion cells in the average person's brain. Each neuron has anything from 1,000 to 100,000 connection points. Multiple pieces of data must be simultaneously retrieved from our memory when needed since the human brain stores information in a scattered fashion [35]. They identify patterns using weighted relationships, which enables them to forecast outcomes and resolve challenging issues.

Because of the learning neuroses in our brain, the relationship between inputs and outputs is constantly changing. Unlike traditional programming, which stores data on a dataset', artificial neural networks store data on the entire network. When a few pieces of data at one location vanish, the network continues to function. The following are some benefits of this ANN:

- After ANN training, the knowledge may provide result even with inadequate data. The amount of efficiency lost here depends on how important the information that is absent.
- ANNs must be able to modify themselves, thus it's critical to identify instances and motivate the network to produce the intended results by showing the network these examples. If the event cannot appear in the entire network in all of its aspects, it may generate erroneous output. The network's succession is directly correlated to the selected occurrences.
- An ANN ability to produce output even if one or more of its cells are twisted gives the network fault tolerance.

1.10.1 Adaptive Artificial Neural Networks

An illustration of a neural network that's specifications may be changed continually, structure, or learning process in response to feedback or environmental changes is known as an adaptive artificial neural network. It makes it possible for the neural network to adjust and perform better over time. An artificial neural network may be made adaptive in a number of ways. Artificial neurons are linked among cells in ANNs, and the amount of weight and bias of these interactions may be changed for learning the system. Neural network structure is determined by the arrangement of connections among layers, neuronal activity, alongside the learning activity. Here are some typical methods.

1. Self-organizing Neural Networks: These neural networks, like the Kohonen Self Organizing Map (SOM), may arrange and modify themselves in response to patterns of input. Data visualization and pattern identification tasks are made easier by these networks' ability to group and display data in an extremely low-dimensional environment.

2. Recurrent Neural Networks (RNNs): are made to handle successive input by incorporating techniques for feedback that allow material to endure throughout time increments. Since the system may change its internal configuration based on previous inputs, it is suitable for purposes such as recognition of speech, natural language processing, and time series research.

3. Adaptive Learning Rate: During training, the weights of classic neural networks are updated using a set learning rate. However, the magnitudes and gradients of the weights are used by adaptive learning rate algorithms like AdaGrad, RMSprop, or Adam to modify the learning rate. This modification facilitates more effective convergence and improved management of noisy data or different scales. Instead of employing a fixed learning rate and this is a ML approach that dynamically modifies the learning rate.

4. Dynamic Connectivity and Structure: The architecture of certain adaptive neural networks can be dynamically altered. To adjust to the level of complexity of the problem, Growing Neural Networks (GNN), for instance, begin with a modest number of neurons and progressively add more neurons or connections during training. Conversely, pruning approaches simplify the network topology and lower processing needs by dynamically eliminating unnecessary connections or neurons.

5. Learning via Reinforcement: It is possible to teach artificial neural networks to communicate with the surroundings and get rewards or penalties depending on their behaviors in reinforcement learning situations. To optimize the cumulative reward, the parameters of the network are modified in response to the feedback that is received. The network can discover the best tactics for difficult decision-making tasks thanks to this adaptive process.

These instances show that artificial neural networks may be made adaptable. The specific problem subject matter, the constitution of the information, and other factors all influence the choice of adapting strategy and the desired adaption tendency. The flexibility of adaptive neural networks allows them to continuously enhance their performance and adjust to changing conditions, which makes them appropriate for a variety of dynamic and non-stationary tasks. Time series prediction, Pattern recognition, robotics, data mining, and other fields where the capacity to adjust and learn from shifting surroundings is essential find use for adaptive neural networks [34]. Because the model may take greater steps in flat portions of the cost distribution and fewer in steep sections, adjusting the teaching rate speeds up the learning procedure.

Differentiating between the nature of network traffic and its functions, like penetration, is more challenging. Differentiating between typical and offensive behaviors takes longer. The framework should be able to process and make decisions at a pace that is equal or greater than the speed at which information arrives in order to handle a huge volume of data without experiencing performance issues or dropping data. As a result, for systems placed in high-speed networks, operating speed is crucial. Additionally, the entire system must have real-time functionality by starting a reaction mechanism as soon as an assault is identified [33].

1.11 Research Gaps

Despite substantial advances in IDS several research gaps remain. Current models generalizability is limited by their reliance on datasets such as NSL_KDD may not adequately capture the complexity of contemporary, real-world networks. While solutions reduce false alarms and enhance detection accuracy, dealing with unknown or zero-day assaults remains difficult. Furthermore, these methodologies are largely focused on benchmark datasets and do not provide evaluation in dynamic, high-traffic contexts where adaptation and real-time processing are required.

Furthermore, the false alarm rate remains an issue in large-scale networks because particularly tiny percentages can cause major disruptions. Existing technologies also fall short of utilizing newer, more complex designs like reinforcement and transformers learning to improve adaptability and efficiency. Furthermore, the scalability and computational overhead of these types of models in applications in real life are unknown. To close these gaps, solid, adaptable, and extensible models that has been verified on a variety of datasets.

1.12 Objectives

The proposed work's objectives are to create a system that efficiently manages selection of features with high accuracy, hybrid classification with optimal care data, and data security. The following is an outline among the planned work's goals.

1. To develop a hybrid Intrusion Detection Model using Crow Search and Artificial Neural Network (ANN) to detect the malicious activities.

2. To enhanced accuracy of Intrusion Detection System through Random Forest Algorithm and Crow Search Optimization.

3. To achieve improved detection accuracy of Intrusion Detection System using hybrid Ant Colony Optimization (ACO) and ANN methodologies.

4. To evaluate the performance metric of Intrusion Detection system using Ant Colony Optimization and Association Rule Mining (ARM).

1.12.1 Roadmap of Objectives

The literature review identifies key research gaps in existing Intrusion Detection Systems, particularly in optimization efficiency, feature selection, and detection accuracy. To address these gaps, the present study formulates targeted research objectives that are systematically addressed in the subsequent chapters.

Chapter 3 focuses on addressing the first research objective by proposing a hybrid Intrusion Detection System that integrates Crow Search Optimization with an Artificial Neural Network (ANN). This chapter details the model architecture, optimization strategy, and detection mechanism employed to identify malicious activities effectively.

Chapter 4 addresses the second research objective by enhancing the accuracy of the Intrusion Detection System through the combined application of the Random Forest algorithm and Crow Search Optimization. The chapter emphasizes feature optimization, model training, and accuracy improvement over existing approaches.

Chapter 5 is dedicated to the third research objective, where an improved IDS framework is developed using a hybrid Ant Colony Optimization (ACO) and ANN methodology. This chapter discusses the optimization of ANN parameters using ACO and evaluates the resulting improvement in detection accuracy.

Chapter 6 addresses the fourth research objective by evaluating the performance metrics of the Intrusion Detection System using Ant Colony Optimization and Association Rule Mining (ARM). A comprehensive performance analysis is presented, covering metrics such as accuracy and false alarm rate.

1.13 Summary

An extensive overview of IDS's is given in this chapter, which also examines the variety of designs and technological kinds used in this industry. An overview of the clustering techniques used for arranging the data is provided, as well as a detailed look at the dataset used in this investigation. The chapter also explores feature selection, highlighting how important it is to improving IDS effectiveness. The chapter additionally discusses the basic ideas of adaptable ANN that serve as the foundation for a large number of contemporary IDS's. The debate expands to include uses of ANN in identifying and addressing different types of malware and assaults. An analysis of the issue description, which outlines the particular difficulties this research attempts to solve, brings this chapter to a close. he objectives and contributions to the current defense body of information are explained in depth, summarizing the importance of the results and its ramifications for further study and use in IDS, while also highlighting how the proposed approach addresses existing research gaps and enhances practical intrusion detection performance, thereby supporting future advancements in secure network systems.

1.14 Organization of the Thesis

The following chapters comprise the structure of the thesis work:

Chapter 1: An overview of cloud computing, intrusion detection and its function in connectivity are covered in this chapter. Also explains the different kinds of IDS's and the features of attacks that go along with them. The part that optimization techniques and cloud computing play in intrusion detection is covered in detail. This chapter provides an overview of the complete thesis endeavor, including the issue statement, purpose, and investigation accomplishment.

Chapter 2: Discusses the various techniques used to identify malicious network vulnerabilities. Several methods of study that carry out intrusion detection and guarantee network and computer security are covered in this chapter. This section also describes the variety of optimization techniques used by different researchers.

Chapter 3: Describes an improved hybrid intrusion detection using CSO and ANN improved techniques for attack detection. This chapter examines the portion of the impact the design of the suggested study; the results show the excellent performance of the implemented model.

Chapter 4: This chapter describe the CSO also combine with Random Forest algorithm for the detection of attack using NSL_KDD dataset. And also compare the results with the existing system. The outcomes demonstrate how well the deployed model performed.

Chapter 5: Provides the description of hybrid classification using ANN-ACO for IDS with clustering algorithm to enhance the identification. This chapter elaborately explains the remaining part of the contribution of research which uses clustering algorithm of intrusion detection for NSL_KDD datasets.

Chapter 6: Describes the performance of a hybrid classifier ARM-ACO for intrusion detection on NSL_KDD datasets, and also compare the results with the existing system. The results show the excellent performance of the implemented model.

Chapter 7: Provides the study work's concluding remarks and the potential for future research expansion.

CHAPTER 2

LITERATURE SURVEY

One component of the information security and computer model is an IDS. Its primary goal is to differentiate between the system's normal operations and its traits, which can be classified as suspicious or malevolent. IDSs are necessary because of the increasing number of incidents that are reported each year and the ongoing advancements in attack techniques. IDS techniques fall into two main categories: anomaly detection and misuse. The abuse detection mechanism is predicated on the idea that an intrusion can be detected by contrasting the current behavior with a set of malicious patterns, which are typically provided by experts or underground websites. State transition analysis, keystroke tracking, and expert systems, are examples of misuse detection. Systems that detect anomalies assume that an intrusion must cause the system to behave differently from how it normally does. Statistical methods, neural networks, association rules, and predictive pattern formation are some of the techniques that enable the application of this technology. Many researches have been conducted in the past regarding computer hacking detection; a number of the more recent ones are covered above [11].

2.1 Different Intrusion Detection System Methods

One-dimensional Convolutional Neural Networks (CNN) based deep learning is recommended for network intrusion detection. While Port Scan falls under the category of passive attacks, DoS Hulk, DDoS, and DoS-GoldenEye are examples of network incursions that fall under the active attack type. The CIC-IDS2017 benchmark dataset was employed [25]. To classify network anomalies, one type of anomaly identification was network intrusion identification [24]. Because it is working with more irrelevant features, it results in low precision.

A CNN-BiLSTM detection and prevention framework for massive networks. To fill the gap in the quantity of category data, the model oversamples the unbalanced data set. To realize the concept of optimization, it is predicated on the integration, collaboration, and selectivity of techniques and techniques in the system for intrusion detection. Pre-processing the data items in real-world application has been shown to be challenging.

Using the CIC-IDS2017 dataset to benchmark machine learning presentations for anomaly-based intrusion detection schemes [6]. To create benchmark results that reveal the most successful AIDS techniques, parameters, and testing criteria, it looks at earlier AIDS research using a set of metrics with different datasets. Additionally, ten consecutive supervised and unsupervised machine learning techniques were examined to determine the most effective ML-AIDS networks. One important factor in AIDSs was time complexity; when assessing the performance efficacy of ML-AIDS, testing and training time also had to be considered. When the regularity of the data items changes, it misses a small number of false alerts. The sound of intrusion indicates a revolutionary approach for spotting network intrusions. This technique uses deep learning-powered sophisticated audio and voice recognition algorithms, starting with the conversion of traffic flow data into waveforms to identify unwanted access. Convolutional neural networks, deep belief systems, and long short-term memory models were amongst the methods of deep learning that are employed. The proposed method was tested on the CIC-IDS2017 and NSL_KDD dataset [14].

An intelligent network intrusion detection system using a combined meta-classifier technique that utilizes recurrent deep learning is introduced [26]. In order to identify and classify network attacks using deep learning-based recurrent modes, the end-to-end method was introduced. To identify the superior features, the suggested method first separates the secret layers of recurrent forms features and then uses kernel-based principal component analysis for feature selection. The greatest properties of recurrent modes were fused to create an ensemble meta-classifier, which was utilized to categorize data. The method for categorizing networks is challenging, and each network's performance varies according to the input data.

2.2 Detecting Intrusions in Clustered Data

The KMC+NBC are a combination of the K-Means Clustering and Naive Bayes Classifier. The data set was labeled and grouped into groups of clusters based on its statistical pattern using a clustering approach [83].

The data clustering was subsequently organized into the correct groupings using NBC. According to the findings, KMC+NBC improves detection rate, accuracy, and the proportion of false alarms by up to 98.79%, 98.99%, and 2.19%, consequently, while lowering the false alarm rate. Table 2.1 displays the comparison of different ids optimization techniques.

Table 2.1: Comparison of Different Intrusion Detection Systems

S. No	Model	Disadvantages	Advantages
1	CNN-BiLSTM [79]	Preprocessing the data objects is challenging when implementing in the real world.	Better efficiency
2	One-dimensional CNN [80]	Limited accuracy as it handles a greater number of unimportant features.	It gives high accuracy
3	The intrusion detection system using LSTM [81]	Low precision.	Improved accuracy
4	Recurrent deep learning-base feature fusion ensemble meta- classifier [82]	The entire network performs differently based on its source data, and categorization its difficult task.	Improved accuracy
5	Benchmarking ML [2]	Few false alarms are missed when there is a shift in the data objects regularity.	Improved accuracy

QALO-K is a successful a combination clustering approach that blends quantum-inspired ant-lion optimization with k-means. This malware detection method was tested using the enormous dataset's from the KDD Cup 99. The outcomes of the simulation indicate that techniques may be successfully used for data clustering and identifying breaches. Convolutional Neural Network (CNN) is used in a revolutionary approach that gives a computer network an efficient way to analyze network traffic for indications of hostile behavior [80]. The fundamental concept involves using a 2D CNN framework to train network flow representation as a 2D image. These innovations are using both aspects of the clustering process and the closest neighbor search to derive an image that represents the network flows. The proposed technique beats rival intrusion detection methods when it comes to of expected accuracy across three baseline data sets. Rotation-DPeak, an enhanced DPeak, was presented based on the straightforward premise that a point p should have a greater density δ, if its density is higher in order to choose p as a density peak, and proposed a variant detection approach to identify anomalous information. This proposed method has been shown to have a good accuracy rating.

The Block chain-Assisted Cluster-based IDS (BAC-IDS) technique is a successful intrusion detection technique created for the IIoT [84]. For the purpose of detecting invasions and enable blockchain-based secure data transmission, the suggested BAC-IDS model clusters IIoT devices. To select the Cluster Heads (CH) and build clusters appropriately, the BAC-IDS technique uses a clustering technique based on Harris Hawks Optimization (HHO). Moreover, intrusion detection based on Chicken Swarm Optimization with Gated Recurrent Units is used to identify the existence of intrusions in an IIoT context. The experimental findings demonstrate how superior the suggested BAC-IDS technology is to the state-of-the-art methods now in use [84]. Deep Evolving Stream Clustering IDS (DESC-IDS) is a deep learning framework for maintaining flow clustering which incorporates stream group with a Sparse Regularization Convolutional Auto-Encoder (SRCAE), designed especially for an in-vehicle IDS. This approach creates a low-dimensional, uneven spatial-temporal projection from data with multiple dimensions by compressing continuously moving signals into 2-D data structures that are analyzed by the SRCAE under the Time Varying Convolutional Network (TCN).

A new Invasion Weed Optimization process is presented by utilizing environmentally friendly Clustered in Conjunction with a Deep Wavelet Neural Network for attack identification (IWOEEC-DWNN) in Vehicle Ad-hoc Networks (VANET). The IWOEEC-DWNN method focuses on the grouped VANET in order to identify potential intrusions. Furthermore, the optimal cluster design and Cluster Head (CH) selection of an IWO-based

...ster approach are used in the IWOEEC-DWNN method to construct clusters. The IWOEEC-DWNN method's effectiveness was tested through extensive calculations [85].

An intrusion detection system for cloud and online computing environments. The best features are chosen for additional detection using Modified Moth Flame Optimization (MMFO) [86] stands for customized manta-ray foraging optimizer. A combination Teacher-Learning-driven Deep Recurrent Neural Network (TL-DRNN) has been created to categorize invasions within a web-cloud scenario. Comparing the suggested IDS scheme's performance against that of current IDS schemes reveals improved outcomes.

IoT-enabled communications, apps, and technologies are used in smart cities to boost operational effectiveness, enhance the quality of service provided by service providers, and enhance the welfare and standard of living of residents. Security threats and attacks are increasing in number along with the growing prevalence of smart city networks. The network of a smart city is vulnerable to threats and attacks since it consists of sensors and big cloud servers. Methods for preventing assaults that cause IoT device faults must be developed [40].

2.3 Cyber-Attack Detection Survey

In order determine malicious behavior, an attack monitoring study examines existing methods, data sources, and difficulties. With the development of new technology to counter more complex and resilient assaults, the area is always changing. Detection techniques, important methodologies such as machine learning and deep learning, typical study datasets, and current research gaps are all covered in detail. Intruders can modify or take ownership of public facilities by inserting destructive software or information into networks that are not adequately safeguarded.

The traffic movement framework was created via an Internet Relay Chat (IRC), and its correctness in capturing actual network activity was assessed by comparing it to the information flow. Cooperative behavior of botnets may be measured using relationship, response, and sync metrics. Coordination among the nodes seemed to be sluggish in this strategy [40]. It exploit weaknesses in computer networks, past technologies, and linked devices to compromise critical services, extract information, and wreak havoc on society.

Table 2.2: Comparative Study of Clustered Data Intrusion Detection

S. No.	Model	Disadvantages	Advantage
1	QALO-K [86]	The models explanation was unclear.	Efficient for intrusion detection and data clustering
2	KMC (K-Means clustering) + NBC (Naive Bayes Classifier) [83]	High time complexity	Improves accuracy, false alarm, and detection rate
3	Rotation-DPeak Algorithm [88]	Unbalanced intrusion data detection is not a good use for this.	Accuracy with good performance
4	CNNs (Convolutional Neural Networks) [79]	This approach ignores potential patterns in the data.	Better predictive accuracy
5	SRCAE (Sparse Regularization Convolutional Auto-Encoder) [89]	It's only good against known attacks.	Enough real-time competitiveness and performance
6	BAC-IDS for IIoT technique [90]	Low false alarm time	High precision and accuracy
7	IDS utilizing deep wavelet neural networks for aggressive plant management [91]	Lot of overhead	Superior to alternative approaches on multiple distinct metrics.

Table 2.2 display the different study of clustered data intrusion detection. Malware binaries are gathered from the Internet using network honey nets as part of a signature-based detection technique [59]. If malware is found, the phoning home communication is automatically monitored. Every malware binary file that has been gathered is run repeatedly to identify malicious communication patterns. Although the suggested approach was secure, it was unable to keep an eye on every device.

In 2006, Binkley and Singh [92] paired IP hosts found in an IRC chat with IPs that were scanning to assess whether they were harmful. Packet drop was particularly high in this area. During the bot infection phase, an internal host communicates with one or more external entities.

A loosely ordered proposed communication flow model to compare potential infections. There are algorithms that can identify botnets based on their many crowd-like activities (e.g. spamming, scanning, and binary downloading), according to Botsnifffer. The computing time of the proposed Asynchronous communication method seems to be greater than it should be. Clustering and cross-correlation of observed C&C server traffic and malicious behaviors were used to enhance the Botsnifffer detection system. Consistency and universality among the nodes were good, but the authentication mechanism was shoddy. A supervised machine learning-based flow-based detection technique for identifying patterns in botnet network traffic [88].

Artificial Neural Networks (ANN) [58] is used to evaluate a system designed to counteract the risks associated with IoT. DDoS/DOS assaults were identified according to the danger categorization and common IoT behaviors. A hypothetical Internet of Things (IoT) situation was used to evaluate the ANN technique's effectiveness. It was able to differentiate between various assault kinds and performed quite well. The model needs a substantial quantity of details with the goal to keep the level of precision high. A two-tier method of classification and Dimension Reduction (DR) are used to identify acts of malicious intent Remote to Login (R2L) and User to Root (U2R). The high-dimensional dataset has been successfully reduced to a lower-dimensional one having minimal properties using linear discrimination and component analysis of DR. Using the Nave Bayes variation on K-Nearest Neighbor and the Certainty Factor, a two-tiered assessment was carried out to identify suspicious behavior.

The model suggested here fared better than earlier models designed to identify R2L and U2R attacks, according to statistics determined by the NSL_KDD dataset. Using the suggested classifier could lead to over fitting [47].

Two components make up the proposed system: the classifier entity and the pre-processing entity. SVM [88] is used to extract and choose traffic flows for usage in the first step, classifying them as either hazardous or non-malicious. Before choosing the winner, they compared and analyzed eight distinct types of extensively supervised machine learning. Thus, the most effective classifiers were C4.5, rTree, and rForest. To identify spam generated by botnets, it was assumed that these networks typically send out massive volumes of spam in short lengths of time. The primary flaw in both systems was the seeming difficulty of warning of an attack.

A security model created with consideration for network layer requirements and IoT characteristics. In a study that accurately characterized indicative detector behaviors using a sensor-DNA profile (S-DNA), it was shown that Anomaly Behavior Analysis (ABA) was able to recognize recent as well as past attacks with a smaller percentage of false positive alarms (4.20%) and a greater detection rate. And for recognized assaults, a correct attack categorization of 98.0% was created and it could reach 95.0 percent accuracy for unknown attacks. Real Alert is an IoT sensing techniques designed for security, reliability, and policy-centricity [93].

The reliability of the IoT devices and data was assessed based on their declared histories and the fact that they were acquired in compliance with policy guidelines. The real alert includes data collection, policy administration, malicious node identification, and trust management. Data and IoT sensor nodes have come to trust real alert's technology, based on actual results. The intrusion detection system cannot assess forwarded packets. After being thoroughly logged into the dataset's, the traffic characteristics of every request were then obtained. As a result, obtained feature states and actions that contributed to establishing the dependability of the information that was protected were used to evaluate the quality [93].

For IoT-related directing assaults like sinkhole and selected forward assaults, an IDS that combines the components for identification that depend on anomalies and specifications was suggested [78]. The system in question used a voting method to identify questionable activity. A well-known platform was used to assess this hybrid approach's efficacy in a smart city setting. According to the simulation data, whenever sinkhole and selectively transmitting attacks occurred simultaneously, that combination of techniques resulted in a True Positive Rate (TPR) of 76.19% and a False Positive Rate (FPR) of 5.92%. This implies restricted store capabilities.

Adopting an IDS-based IoT framework, the viability of using standard hardware as the mainstay of the suggested architecture was investigated. The Raspberry Pi is currently the most widely used single-board computer. Its performance was assessed using an open-source intrusion detection system named Snort. Using devices with restricted resources such as the Raspberry Pi, the proposed approach may provide excellent protection for IoT dispersed systems, corresponding to the trials. The main flaw in the IDS was the fact that it allowed an attacker to damage a target system [40].

Processing data relating to health may reduce the likelihood of malware attacks. The DNN was mainly utilized to examine the IoT device in order to confirm its legitimacy. The possibility of over fitting seems to be a greater disadvantage in this instance than in others. To detect a range of severe network-centered intrusions in IoT networks, several IDS layers have been developed using a supervised techniques [71].

Every IoT device connected to the internet could be categorized and analyzed by the framework, which could also identify illicit packets and categorize various attack types. Eight renowned industrial devices were used to evaluate the technology in a smart-home environment. The core functions of the system produced 90.01%, 98.10%, and 96.11% of the F-measures. In this instance, the extremely high degree of security came at a greater implementation cost [93].

An intelligent framework built around improved and simulated genetic algorithms was developed for deep neural networks-centric anomaly network IDSs [26], which automatically builds an efficient hybridized optimization model. Several of these techniques were utilized to determine the best way to combine the most crucial elements that go into building DNN-centered IDS or to affect how well it performs. These elements are FS, the architecture of the DNN, data normalization, and momentum and activation functions. This ensures a higher detection rate and precision while reducing the number of false alerts. The results of the research demonstrated its superiority over current systems as well as its ability to identify intrusions with greater detection precision and a lower percentage of false alarms. Although they are meant to prevent an attack before it reaches any kind of network systems, network-based intrusion detection systems offer a major benefit. DoS attacks on the other hand are unavoidable.

An algorithm for a smart city IDS framework known as Restricted Boltzmann Machines (RBMs) [94]. RBMs were used because of unsupervised learning and the capability of controlling real-time representations from smart meters and sensors. These features were then used to train different classifiers. A smart irrigation unit was used to test and assess the methodology's performance. The results demonstrated how the structure could identify assaults with greater accuracy. Additionally, it scored better than the classification approach that omitted the feature learning stage. One significant flaw in this approach is that it appears to be highly dependent on hardware. In this instance, a small 3.120% error rate enhanced the malware detection rate was 98.7%. When compared to existing methods, this method has a notable error rate.

Using selecting features with Naive Bayes approach, this combination of methods for malware detection creates an ideal SVM by identifying exceptions and reducing the total size of the input data set. Following that, the analysis is performed using a prioritized KNN-based classifier [32].

There are some approaches which consist of some modules: the Decision Making Module (DMM), the Feature Selection Module (FSM), and the Data Preprocessing Module (DPM). This model selects relevant attributes based on accuracy, testing time, and training time by recognizing mutual and feature effects. The main flaw in the given model is that it does not accurately represent the traffic patterns of today because the author used outdated datasets to evaluate its efficacy. Additionally, machine learning approaches are more effective and efficient than the methods the author describes. Many specialists have suggested methods to boost detection rates by balancing the dataset because many intrusion datasets are skewed.

The Synthetic Minority Over-sampling Technique (SMOTE) oversampling approach was used to construct a model [25] [72].

IDS are frequently created using ML-based techniques [21]. When creating anomaly-based intrusion detection systems, the term classification with in this manner encompasses machine learning methods that differentiate among safe and dangerous behaviors in internet traffic information collecting. It was suggested that an intrusion detection system employs an ensemble classifier and feature selection [47]. An ensemble approach based on Forest by Penalizing Attributes (Forest PA), C4.5, and Random Forest (RF), which includes an Average of Probabilities Algorithm, for multi-attack classification. The ensemble technique is called CFS-BA, and it uses correlations to select features. They asserted that the classifier has 99% accuracy for both the dataset. The investigator's failure to consider the time efficiency of this model is a significant flaw in the system. An integrated intrusion system that employs KNN classifiers with prioritized improved SVM [32] continuously following datasets for attack identification system: NSL_KDD, KDD Cup99, and Koyotto 2006+.

In accordance with the mean sample size, the crooked style samples are expanded. They assert that they achieved a 99% accuracy rate with this technique Linear Discriminant Analysis (LDA) by utilizing RF, Ad-boost, KNN, and DT [53]. In intrusion detection models, methods like the Genetic Algorithm (GA) are frequently employed. The approach is not tested using time-based metrics, despite the article's claim of 99% accuracy [46].

A model was subjected to the classification approach known as Genetic Approach Support Vector Machine (GASVM) [46]. To pick features, a hybrid approach is used. The selected features are given three priorities by the GA. These characteristics are used for further classification. Several deep learning methods are also suggested for creating effective IDS. In order to construct the framework, a Long Short Term Memory (LSTM) neural network and an adaptive method to anomaly detection. The information came from the most recent CIC-IDS2017 dataset. Despite achieving a 96.2% correctness rate, the model's computational speed of execution was not evaluated. The CIC-IDS 2017 dataset serves as the basis for an artificial neural network identification system that reports a detection accuracy of 99.97% and a standard Receiver Operating Characteristic (ROC) curve value of 0.999% [25].

Although the model had an impressive 99.97% accuracy rate, its sole purpose was to identify botnets. Furthermore, the system's spatial performance is not assessed. The Deep Neural Network (DNN) [26] and Spectral Clustering (SC) techniques served as the foundation for the proposal of SCDNN. It was evaluated using the NSL_KDD datasets, sensor network, and KDD-Cup99. The disadvantage of the SCDNN is that it necessitates setting the DNN layers weight and thresholds parameters as well as determining the clusters k and parameters through empirical observation rather than hypothetical. Additionally, time efficiency and the technique's effectiveness are evaluated using old datasets. Of the stated model is not measured. Several deep learning approaches were contrasted [28].

The approaches that were evaluated employing the CIC-IDS2018 dataset included recurrent neural networks, deep belief networks, limited Boltzmann machines, and deep auto encoders. There was just 5% of the entire dataset used for this research. Only the accuracy and recall rate of deep neural networks were evaluated. Measures like accuracy rate and F-measure were not included of the evaluation. Two recurrent neural networks, a feed-forward component, and a restricted Boltzmann machine make up the recently created DNN model.

Model training was operated on the CIC-IDS2018 dataset. This dataset's severe skewness was not corrected by any method. This method did not yield any findings for the CIC-IDS2018 dataset contains a few attack groups. The recently suggested distributed deep learning technique is used by both HIDS and NIDS or to detect attacks [72]. Scale-Hybrid-IDS-AlertNet (SHIA), is a security system for intrusion detection designed to identify scaled hybrid attacks. The methodology that was described did not employ any attempt to make the 2018 CIC-IDS dataset more balanced, which seemed to be severely skewed. The results of this strategy showed disappointing outcomes for a few assault categories. To improve the IDS effectiveness, some authors also use sophisticated learning algorithms like Extreme Learning and Particle Swarm Optimization (PSO) [67]. Novel Framework suggests two technologies for adaptive systems, such as extreme machine learning and clustering techniques for cooperative detection systems for network intrusions.

The Selection Maker, Updating Administrator, and Clusters Administrator are the three primary parts of an intrusion detection system. Whenever the modifications manager gets a request for a modification, the individual making the decision considers various alternatives, including the way the clustered manager arranges the training data. The antiquated NSL_KDD dataset was used to evaluate the approach that depends on PSO and the Fast Learning Model (FLM). The KDD99 dataset is used to evaluate this model's effectiveness. However, the framework's behavioral effectiveness hadn't been assessed, and the approach failed to identify all types of attacks. SVM, KNN, PSO is an aggregation approach that has been suggested for the detection of intrusions. Each expert has access to five binary classification algorithms, and the additions of each specialized are taken into account in each course. For every observation, the specialist's classification algorithm votes, and an evenly weighted plurality voting technique is used to aggregate the results from multiple experts. Moreover, Light GBM-based intrusion detection systems in both sequential and real-time are being presented. This approach maintains the accuracy of assault detection while utilizing two time-saving techniques. First, as part of the intrusion detection process, it makes use of a light gradient boosting machine, or Light GBM. Second, successive detection of breaches is an efficient way to evaluate traffic data.

Concurrent intrusion detection methods including integration and interaction complexity form the foundation of Swift IDS. Furthermore, this approach can maintain stability at network rates of up to 1.26 Gbps [36]. The speed at which a query may be classified as harmful or benign has not been evaluated in prior research. User interface and performance of the system might be seriously hampered by categorization procedure latencies.

Classifiers based on the Feature Selection (FS) and SVM methodology were examined, along with algorithmic classification methods for intrusion detection [116]. Using techniques based on soft computing, having trouble in identifying attacks throughout the inquiry has additionally highlighted. For FS and feature transformation, particle swarm optimization, or PSO, was applied.

The NSL_KDD Cup 99 assault dataset uses SVMs for choosing characteristics subsequent intrusion categorization. We used the Fisher discriminant rate technique to show classifications using Self-Organized Map (SOM) and feature selection using 17 attributes from the dataset. In addition to FS and Decision tree (DT) for classification, the cuttlefish algorithm for optimization is provided for intrusion detection [51]. This method lowers the rate of false alarms while improving accuracy and TPR. A dataset's presented FS utilizing a classification tree and regression employing a Bayesian network to assess the effectiveness and detection accuracy of the IDS on KDD Cup 99 [12]. The various datasets are thoroughly examined employing a range of ML and data mining approaches, including SOM, DT, K-Means, and SVM. Many classification models, influencing multiple, ensemble, and single classifiers, are described in the study. IDS was used to a cloud system that used a variety of classifiers, such as DT, Bayesian, and associative.

We compare many previous methods that use clustering techniques, matching datasets, classification strategies, machine learning techniques, and other investigative systems and detection mechanisms [17]. This offers a distinctive contribution by highlighting the necessity of an improved automated intelligent hybrid IDS model built on cutting-edge machine learning approaches, which would increase accuracy while reducing false alarm rates.

Attacks using targeted advanced persistent threats analyze the host user's 30 behavioral patterns using an 83-dimensional vector, where each characteristic represents a different way; the person behaves [18]. The method was designed to determine how frequently each behavior occurs for each activity. To distinguish between dangerous and typical occurrences, a method for categorizing data was established using a C4.5 decision tree. Each new sample was evaluated in reference to the tree.

2.4 Summary

In intrusion detection systems, a critical area of research is figuring out the best and most effective attention measure for classifiers and feature detectors according to optimization. Reviews of an intrusion detection system that employed moth-flame optimization, deep learning-based hybrid optimization, adaptive optimization, nature-inspired optimization, and extreme learning machines an improved algorithm for binary manta ray foraging, and particle swarm optimization were also included in the literature. Intrusion detection can directly benefit from a variety of clustering approaches. The factors of accuracy, specificity, sensitivity, and precision. F-Measure and Recall are the measuring matrices for IDS. Since few interest measures deal with noise issues and reactivity to occurring of a rule's consequence, a desire measure that resolves the previously mentioned issues is essential.

CHAPTER 3

AN IMPROVED HYBRID INTRUSION DETECTION USING CROW SEARCH AND ARTIFICIAL NEURAL NETWORK

As computer networks continue to develop, serious worries about security and vulnerability have emerged. IDS are used by network managers to provide crucial safety for systems. Recent IDS systems create false alerts triggered by normal user behaviors instead of identifying fresh attacks. This issue potentially resolved and detection accuracy raised with the usage of neural networks. To identify anomalies, we provide a hybrid method in this chapter that combines neural networks with correlation-based feature selection. The typical dataset NSL_KDD is used for experimental research on intrusion detection utilizing contemporary attacks. A new Hybrid Crow Search Analysis Optimization with an Artificial Neural Network (HCSAOANN) is proposed. According to the results, it performs better with regards to of excellent recall, F1-Score, accuracy, and precision. In this chapter a combination of improved Crow Search Analysis (CSA) approach with Crow Search Optimization (CSO) along with Artificial Neural Network (ANN) that may come together into the general optimal outcome in the search function, to investigate the feature space in the recommended HCSAOANN algorithm. Specific performance criteria's are applied in this approach, which employed an artificial ANN as a classifier. In comparison to the prior fuzzy technology, the HCSAOANN methodology much better by achieving 98% precision rate and 98% accuracy. This is 8.87% better than the FC-ANN technique and 2.2% greater than the earlier CSO-ANFIS technique.

3.1 Introduction

Businesses are increasingly presenting themselves to a variety of digital dangers as an expense for insight processing and Internet connectivity declines. According to research by the Computer Emergency Response Team/Coordination Centre (CERT/CC) [1], the number of assaults continues to be increasing yearly. It is therefore more important than ever to make our information systems tolerant and resilient to such attacks, especially those that are used for critical operations in the defense and commercial sectors. Identifying malevolent activities that jeopardize the integrity, confidentiality, and accessibility of data sources is part of intrusion detection [2]. The foundation of conventional intrusion detection techniques is a deep comprehension of known attack signatures. When events are watched, intrusions are detected by comparing them against signatures [3]. These techniques evaluate the values of attributes and detect breaches by using information from a number surveillance sources and a set of detrimental activities supplied by individuals with expertise [4]. The identity dataset's must be maintained regularly as soon as a new kind of intrusion is discovered. One major weakness in signature-based techniques is that they cannot detect emerging cyber threats, which are started using novel strategies [5]. A novel assault may occasionally take a long time to spread throughout systems, regardless of when it has been identified and its distinctive characteristics developed. Because of these limitations, the adoption of methods for detection of breaches that utilize data mining is increasing [7].

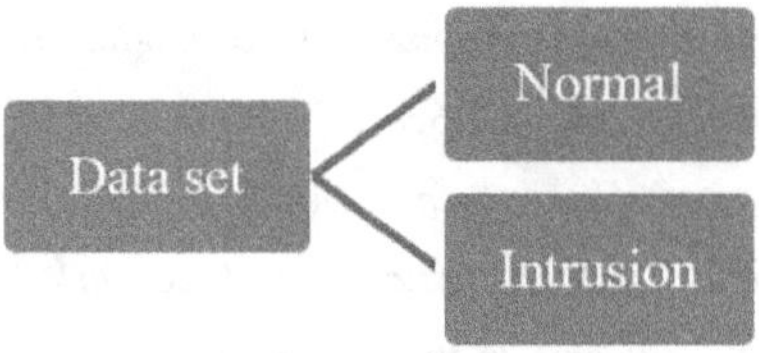

Figure 3.1: Categories in Dataset

Anomaly detection and abuse detection are the two categories into which data mining techniques for intrusion detection are frequently divided. Every instance in such a dataset is classified into two categories: "intrusion" and "normal" as seen in Figure 3.1, after then, the indexed data is used to train a machine learning system [7]. These methods can continually train up systems for intrusion detection utilizing a variety of input data, including the most recent attack types, provided that the attacks have been correctly tagged. One clear benefit of using abuse detection techniques is that they can accurately identify known assaults and their variations. One obvious flaw in systems is their inability to detect dangers whose events weren't yet noticed. Anomaly detection, on the other hand, builds models of typical behavior and automatically identifies one deviation from all of this, classifying the latter as unusual. Anomaly detection systems detect new invasions by identifying departures from typical usage patterns. Despite having effective detection systems, one potential disadvantage of deploying them is the potential for false alarms. Because of its vulnerability and prevalence, continuous evaluation is necessary to guarantee cyberspace security [8]. Significant cyberattacks have occurred across the world, including Internet of Things (IoT) attacks [78], corporate espionage, cyber warfare, crypto-jacking attacks, social engineering attacks, and data breaches that allowed attackers to obtain billions of credits or debit card credentials. An IDS is highly recommended together with different safety measures [9].

According to their detection criteria, some IDS act after threats are identified, while others keep an eye on network traffic and send out alerts for questionable activities. Anomaly-based IDS can identify network intrusions by carefully analyzing system behavior and distinguishing between malicious and legitimate activities [10]. Many IDSs use abuse detection techniques, which entail searching for and warning about known patterns of malevolent behavior. The primary disadvantage of this kind of malware detection techniques is that, despite its ability to confine them by searching for existing assaults, it won't be capable to fight opposing upcoming assaults since it lacks signatures. Because of this, there is a serious security flaw in the system that a hacker might easily exploit to fool the IDS. To identify both known and freshly emerging threat signatures, these IDS must be updated on a regular basis. To add intelligence to IDS, ML and DL techniques are frequently used [11]. These techniques assist protect the system from possible risks and make it easier to identify different kinds of assaults. But the effectiveness of an algorithm that uses machine learning in identifying breaches depends on choosing the correct dataset.

IDS datasets that are publicly available, including KOYOTO [13], NSL_KDD [14], DARPA [11], and KDD 99 [12], have been used to train and test recent machine learning models. The fact that the suggested statistical-based solutions are out-of-date and do not account for contemporary traffic patterns is a significant drawback. Furthermore, a lot of academics have created ML prototypes for IDS, most of which focus on correctness as the main criterion for evaluating the predictive model. However, as IDS must generate precise predictions in real-time, precision by itself is insufficient to assess a system's efficacy [33][34]. Its goal is to detect possible breaches of security and record information about them so that authorities in security may look into and address them.

Evaluating IDS for prediction accuracy, or prediction latency, is just as important as evaluating accuracy. Although it improves prediction accuracy, the impact on prediction delay has not been studied by most scholars. High-performing IDS, accuracy, and prediction delay should also have a notable actual positive prediction rate. False negatives that are mistakenly classed as benign and false positives that are mistakenly detected as attacks cannot be regarded as equal. Positive results can increase the system's resources, while false negative results can destroy it. Therefore, along with prediction, accuracy, and recall rate, the delay is essential for evaluating the IDS model's performance [43][44].

3.2 Contribution

The following concisely describes the primary contributions of the proposed work:

Given that the dataset produced by NSL contains both quantitative and qualitative information, and because categorical data is challenging to process, the integrated optimization and crowd search analysis algorithm's main advantage is that it considers every feature of the dataset. To enable the identification of attacks, qualitative information is identified using a one-hot encoding technique.

One more advantage of the suggested study is that the feature selection relies on correlation. This correlation-based choices approach must be changed if the dataset varies or if we are dealing with a real-time dataset. To accommodate the complex dataset, we need to adjust the algorithm if we utilize the feature selection method applied in earlier research. The HCSAOANN method outperformed the CSO-ANFIS method by 2.2% and the FC-ANN techniques by 8.877%, achieving a 98% precision and 98% accuracy rate. The feature selection pre-processing stage reduces the complexity of datasets and improves classification performance by selecting the most important characteristics.

3.3 Learning on Valuable Classes

Traditional data mining techniques are inappropriate for abusing detection-related issues because of several special factors, including handling unequal class distribution, learning from data streams, and recognizing network connections. Although the intrusion that's concern, incursion, is considerably more modest and, as a result, more uncommon than the class that represents usual network activities, the issue of an imbalanced distribution of class in intrusion detection for networking is evident. In these situations, where 98% to 99% of the population may behave normally, a fundamental classification that assigns a class label to every member of the class may be close to 98% to 99% accurate. In this instance, the category's accuracy as a standard evaluation metric is insufficient. Evaluating a machine learning model efficacy is essential for the minority group. To determine the model's efficacy, accuracy and precision metrics as well as ROC calculations are used [15]. The effectiveness associated with machines learning systems is often evaluated as shown in Table 3.1 [16].

Table 3.1: Typical Metrics for Assessing (Intrusions)

Performance Matrix		Predicted Correlation Labels	
		Intrusions	Normal
Authentic Correlation Labels	Intrusions	T_P	F_N
	Normal	F_P	T_N

Table 3.1 provides the following definitions for ROC, F1-value, and precision: Because they are based on a series of occurrences, some historical data mining algorithms are better equipped to handle incursions. Algorithms that detect misuse must label all data, but it takes time and a lot of human expertise to categorize connectivity as either legal or intrusive. All these issues make creating anomaly-based models extremely difficult. To learn from non-traditional classes, sophisticated methods of classification have been created. For example, establishing the norms is at the heart of the two-stage learning techniques Positive Learning and Negative Learning (PN Learning) rule [9]. While the subsequent phase finds N-rules and eliminates false alarms generated in the preceding phase, the initial level searches for P-rules which encompass the bulk of obtrusive events. CREDOS [17], is a novel technique that uses ripple-down rules to overfit the training data at first, then prunes it to improve generalization ability. In data mining, it is well known that combining many classifiers can improve prediction accuracy. Including rare class strategies for learning [13] is the goal of the Rare-

Boost [15] methodology. Rare-Boost modifies the importance of occurrence for each of the four items in Table 3.1, as opposed to the usual boosting technique, which appropriately raises the importance of the occurrences. We additionally investigated a traditional association-based categorization method by focusing on an unusual classification challenge. After every category completes the component established process of development, the most effective sets of items are picked as meta-features. These developed features are added to the source data set, and the resultant information set is then put through a typical categorization process. In the existing association-based classification approaches, confidence-like measures are used to select the best rules to include in the classifiers. However, the effectiveness of these techniques may depend on how well each kind is represented in the data collection. As long as they don't have very low precision, several of the incredible accuracy collections could also be useful during unusual class assignments. F-value, ROC, and accuracy are therefore utilized to determine the most suitable items which might be part of the initial set of data. [18][19][20].

3.4 Proposed Work

Now, we are going over the initial CSA-CSO enabling intrusion detection as well as our intended work. The algorithm for the crow search analysis take the inspiration as crow search the food [1]. Each cycle aims at updating the location of every crow. A further randomly picked crow's positioning serves as the basis for this new version. This algorithm maximizes performance and accomplishes goals by utilizing the collective intelligence of the community. These algorithms can imitate the social interactions, communication styles, and decision-making procedures that are typical of crows by analyzing their behavior.

Without a doubt, crows are intelligent animals with big minds for their size that live in flocks. Additionally, they can recall and collect their food even months after it has been hidden. The mirror exam also causes embarrassment for participants. They can maintain their appearance, and if a disagreeable one is spotted, they can use sophisticated communication to let the other crows know. Crows, like other gregarious animals, may rob other crows by spotting where they conceal their nourishment and then taking it. When a crow believes another is pursuing him to deceive a thief, he moves to a new location far from where the food is hidden. The procedure is simple to use and has minimal setting.

3.5 The Framework of CSA

In this case, the total amount of crows (solutions) is represented by NC, and current populations having problem parameters are denoted by pd.

At iteration t *or* $i = 1, 2, 3, \ldots, NC$, the location of every crows i can be expressed by a set of vectors $s_i^t = [s_{i1}^t, s_{i2}^t, \ldots.. s_{ipd}^t]f$, where s_i^t is the likely positional selection in dimensions pd every crow i.

A crow saying, "I actually want to grab something of an alternate crow j." could result in two different outcomes.

1. Crow j does not see crow i, who pursues it; when crow i finds the meal which crow j has hidden, he or she rearranges it according to 3.1.

$$s_i^{t+1} = s_i^t + ri * fm_j^t * (n_j^t - s_i^t) \quad (3.1)$$

where *fm* represents the flight's length and ri represents an arbitrary integer between 0 and 1.

2. Here, i followed herself to discover in which her meals is concealed after realizing she is a crow. To trick the crow i, the crow j in this situation dances irregularly.

Mathematically, the two cases can be concatenated as follows:

$$s_i^{t+1} = \begin{cases} s_i^t + ri * fm_j^t * (n_j^t - s_i^t), & rj \geq AWP_i^t \\ \text{Random position selected,} & \text{Otherwise} \end{cases} \quad (3.2)$$

The crow j's awareness probability at iteration t is AWP_i^t, where the random values are r_i *and* r_j. The ability of crows to search is influenced by the value of FM. Global search is supported by high f_m values, whereas local search is supported by low values [35]. A clearly defined fitness function is used to evaluate each crow as the method is implemented. After that, the crows move around in relation to the fitness value. The viability of each new post is assessed. 3.3 indicate that the birds' memories have been updated:

$$m_i^{t+1} = \begin{cases} s_i^{t+1}, & \text{if } f\, s_i^{t+1} \text{ is better than } f\,(s_i^t) \\ n_i^t, & \text{Otherwise} \end{cases} \quad (3.3)$$

Algorithm 3.1: The CSA

1: The location of Crow is determined at random and is initialized as $s_i^t(1 = 1, 2, 3, \ldots\ldots m)$.

2: AWP and F_m have predetermined values.

3: For the whole crow s_i^t, the fitness function computed $f\,(s_i^t)$.

4: For every crow s_i^t : Memory is set to n_i^s,

(i). set t = 0

(ii). Iterations at maximum level = x

(iii). Crow's flocks = y

5: while (t < x) do

6: for k = 1 to y

7. Choose a crow to follow at random.

8. Provide an awareness probability breakdown.

9: if (r and AWP_k^t)

10: $s_k^{t+1} = s_k^t + rk * fm_k^t * (n_k^t - s_k^t)$

11: else

12: s_k^{t+1} = find a random location in the search field.

13: end

14: end

15: Determine if the new location is viable s_k^{t+1}

16: $f(s_i^{t+1})$ assesses the crow's new location.

17: The crow's memory position is then updated by n_i^{t+1}.

18: end while

19: Created a solution that was optimized.

The present approach for each crow is then updated based on the findings of determining local optima with 3.5 and 3.7.

$$S_i^t = [s_{i,1}^t, s_{i,j}^t, \dots \dots \dots s_{i,d}^t] \qquad i = 1, 2, 3 \dots\dots\dots NC \tag{3.4}$$

$$V_{i,j}^{t+1} = w' v_{i,j}^t + A_1 r_1 (G1best_{i,j}^t - s_{i,j}^t) + A_2 r_2 (G2best_j^t - s_{i,j}^t) \tag{3.5}$$

The variables r_1 and r_2 are random, while A_1 and A_2 stand for the interpersonal and cognitive aspects, respectively. The inertial load of the swarm describes how its prior velocity influences the speed of the next phase or w'. Equation 3.6 states the value of w'.

$$w' = w'_{max} - iteration * \frac{w'_{max} - w'_{min}}{x} \tag{3.6}$$

Where, x = max_iteration

$$S_{i,j}^{t+1} = s_{i,1}^t + V_{i,j}^{t+1} \tag{3.7}$$

3.6 The HCSAOANN (Proposed Algorithm)

The primary actions according to the recommended approach for handling feature selection issues are described in Algorithm 3.2. To create a method that might benefit from its combination, this section also integrates algorithms for ANN with CSA-CSO concepts.

The suggested method targets a small number of crows with the best treats, increasing the efficiency of completely random monitoring all crows in the traditional CSA. The different change places or crow positions within the CSO are then constructed by Algorithm 3.3 using the CSA technique. The goal is to enable both methods to explore the area of search independently, independent of each other's results. Choose the starting setups for variables such as the number of repetitions, likelihood of awareness, duration of flight, size of the flock, and position of the crows, among other parameters related to the crow search. Create a breach forecasting with a network of neurons and a categorization framework. Enhance the memory of the crows utilizing a crow search-based approach following each modification. When compared to the earlier developed the most advanced model, the newly developed heuristic Crow Search Optimization (CSO) technique improved the intrusion accuracy and detection rate whereas lowering its rate of false alarms when utilized to specific characteristics of the NSL_KDD collection. CSA generally needs fewer variables to be tuned than other types of self-learning techniques, which helps streamline the procedure of optimization and minimize the difficulty of determining the ideal parameter values.

Algorithm 3.2: The HCSAOANN

1. Determine the size of the crow, N', and dimensionality D' that matches all of the dataset's properties.

2: Get the A_1, A_2; weight factor w'_{min}, w'_{max} ; Maximum iteration x; Maximum velocity v'_{max}; Awareness probability AWP; flight length f_l'

3: The population for each solution is randomly selected using s_i^t and the velocity of the D-dimensional vector is set to t = 0. As the velocity is set at t = 0, the population is randomly assigned to each solution's D dimensional vector.

4: $w' = w'_{max}$ - iteration * $\frac{w'_{max}-w'_{min}}{x}$

5: The best solutions for each solution are assessed using $f(s_{i,j}^t)$ wherever G1best and G2best have been defined.

6: Initialization of parameters while using ANN, CSA, and CSO.

7. Develop a method for intrusion identification and forecasting using a network of neurons framework.

8: Every time the crow's memory is refreshed, utilize Crow Search-based optimization to improve this framework.

9: The NSL-KDD dataset's selected characteristics were optimized using the Metaheuristic Crow Search (CSO) approach.

10: Use $s_{i,j}^t$ as the broad public, a group of crows that must eat the best food, and a specific quantity of crows to operate CSA.

11: Change the CSA's returning position in reverse using method 3.

12: Update the location of the crows.

13: for l = 1 to XX

14: $V_i^{t+1} = w' v_i^t + A_1 n_{i,1}(G1best_i^t - s_i^t) + A_2 n_{i,2}(G2best_j^t - s_i^t)$

end

for l = 1 to XX

for j = 1 to D

if ($v'(i,j) > V'_{max}$)

$v'(i,j) = V'_{max}$

end

if ($v'(i,j) < -V'_{max}$)

$v'(i,j) = -V'_{max}$

end

$u = \frac{1}{1 + e^{-v'(i,j)}}$

if (rand < u)

$s_{i,j}^{t+1} = 1$

else

$s_{i,j}^{t+1} = 0$

end

end

end

t' = t' + 1

Obtain the Final outcome.

The below figure 3.2 shows the step by step flow of the implemented model using crow search analysis optimization with an artificial neural network.

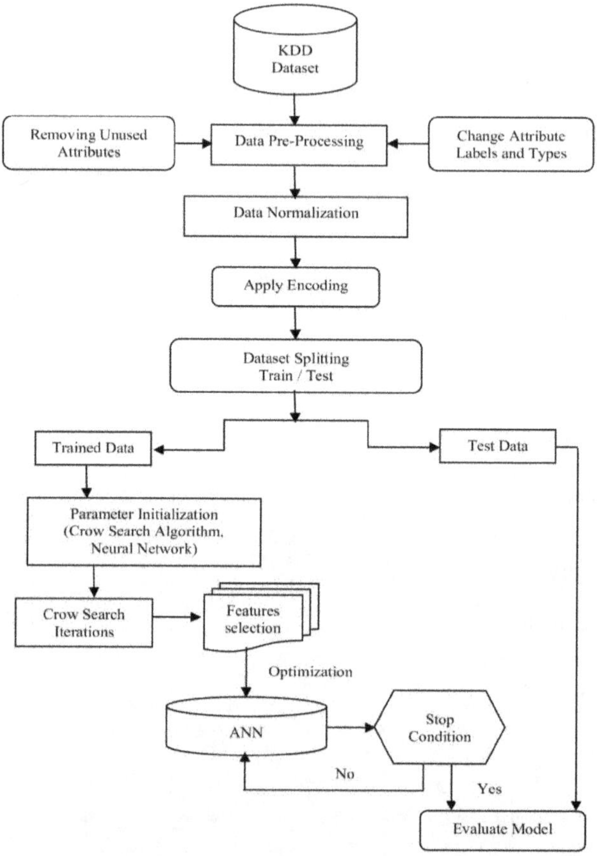

Figure 3.2: HCSAOANN Model

Algorithm 3.3: The location of the crow on the contrary

```
do
    i = 1
        i = i++
    if (f(s_i^t> mincrowt))
        s_i^{t/OPP} = ai + bi - s_i^t
    while (i<=N)
```

Two potentials are typically selected whenever the feature vector has a size N, which is a sizable space for thorough searching. The suggested hybrid algorithm 3.1 and algorithm 3.2 is used to dynamically explore the feature space by achieving this and offering the optimal feature combination. In this case, feature selection needs to meet several goals to get the best outcome, which minimizes the feature subset chosen while also raising the output accuracy of a particular classifier. Figure 3.2 shows the flow chart for the suggested methodology based on crow search optimization.

1. Data pre-processing:

   a. Examine the NSL-KDD dataset.

   b. Since we believe that the attribute "difficulty_level" is not a decision criterion and will not aid in the classification of our dataset, remove it from the dataset.

   c. Assigning the appropriate attack class to the attack labels.

   d. Choosing the dataset's numeric attribute columns.

2. Data Normalization:

   a. Choose a dataset's categorical data attribute.

   b. Using the dataset for this categorical attribute to create a data frame.

   c. Categorize the categorical column features by utilizing the pandas.get_dummies() function, and subsequently apply one-hot encoding to the categorical attributes. After this, incorporate these characteristics into the training models.

3. Selection of Features:

   a. Using only the dependent characteristics from the dataset, identifying those features that have correlations greater than 0.5 with the encoding attack label attribute.

   b. The Pearson correlation coefficient is used to choose attributes.

   c. Including the one-hot-encoded classified information frame with the chosen attribute.

4. Training and Testing:

   a. To get a model that is more precise, the dataset can be split into sets of 75% for training and 25% for testing, or it can be split into additional training and testing sets.

5. Initializing parameters and assessing the model:

a. Set up the crow search parameters, including the position of the crow, Flight length, Flock Size, and Awareness Probability.

Develop a neural network-based model for categorizing and predicting assaults. Each time the crow memory is updated refine this model utilizing crow search. In comparison to leading classifiers, as implemented to the selected characteristics of the NSL_KDD information set, our meta-heuristic CSO approach reduced the false alarm rate while increasing the IDS rate of detection and accuracy.

3.7 Experimental Results

The following phases are used to conduct the observations for this study:

1. Analyzing several attack types in a dataset.

a. Characterization attacks on the NSL_KDD dataset.

b. Classification of the main assaults in the NSL_KDD dataset.

2. Various accuracy against epoch plots for test and training information sets based on neuron count, epochs, and batch size.

a. Display the outcomes of our applications with and without CSA.

b. Assessment of Various Metrics on binary class distribution performance.

c. Assessment of the performance of different multi-class distribution measures.

3.7.1 Dataset

The NSL_KDD was developed as an improved KDD99 to overcome its flaws. The NSL_KDD contains 125,973 training instances, the following data set is available to everyone at https://www.kaggle.com/datasets/hassan06/nslkdd. The train and test sets are first cleared of redundant information. Second, to provide reliable classifier system outputs, alternative records were chosen from the primary KDD99 dataset. Third, an imbalanced probability distribution was no longer an issue. [20][21]. NSL-KDD purposefully regulates the ratio of typical to unusual assault types, in contrast with numerous dataset's that struggle with excessive repetition, to prevent algorithms from achieving inflated efficiency from memorization of regular sequences. It is especially useful for assessing how effectively methods generalized to invisible threats because of the way it is structured, which compels systems of learning to discern minute distinctions among benign and harmful traffic.

3.7.2 Results and Discussion

This research included 20 samples, 60+ revisions, and random procedures. Python was used to implement comparative tactics on an Intel i3-7020U CPU. The results of the validation revealed statistical measures. In this instance, the method's prediction ability is greatly increased by the use of crow search optimization, which enables it to further precisely identify trends as well as abnormalities in intricate dataset's. Scientists and engineers may enhance the accuracy of their systems by using this cutting-edge optimization approach, which will provide more accurate outcomes in a variety of programs, including information security, wherein prompt and accurate identification is essential. Because it provides a variety of datasets accessible to the general public for the evaluation of systems for intrusion detection, the NSL_KDD dataset is essential in this field. Experts collaborate and innovate more as a result of this availability, which eventually makes online spaces safer. Several important problems which have previously hampered the assessment of IDS are addressed by the data collection activities conducted by NSL_KDD. The dataset, for example, lessens the issues of unbalance and duplication that frequently occur in conventional information sets, which can distort the preparation and evaluation procedures. NSL_KDD makes it possible to create more resilient models that can function effectively in real-world situations by offering an even distribution of both regular and attack traffic [22][23].

Among the greatest important advantages of the NSL_KDD data collection is the copious quantity of unnecessary data [24][25]. Because of that, machines are biased in their ability to retain typically and are unable to comprehend distinct libraries that are generally more detrimental to systems, such as R2L and U2R attacks. The NSL_KDD dataset, which comprised 125,973 records including both normal and abnormal instances having 42 attributes and 4 types of features [26].

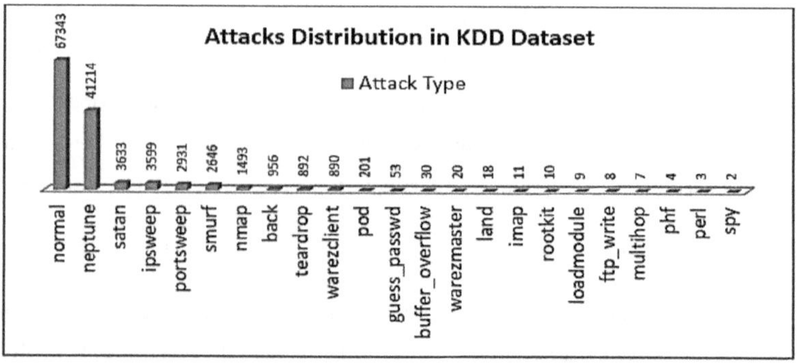

Figure 3.3: KDD Dataset Attacks Distribution

Observing Figure 3.3, it is clear that the distribution of samples across various types of assault is not consistent; indicating that the data set is significantly unbalanced. The sample count of DoS-type assaults is higher than that of U2R-type attacks. This unequal sample distribution may cause issues for any data mining-based classification model. Table 3.2 displays a range of basic attacks through the KDD-Cup dataset. The dataset's many attack types are separated into groups called Probe, Normal, Dos, R2L, and U2R.

Table 3.2: NSL_KDD Dataset Attacks Classification

	Total	Normal	Dos	Probe	R2L	U2R
KDD Dataset	125973	67343	45927	11656	995	52

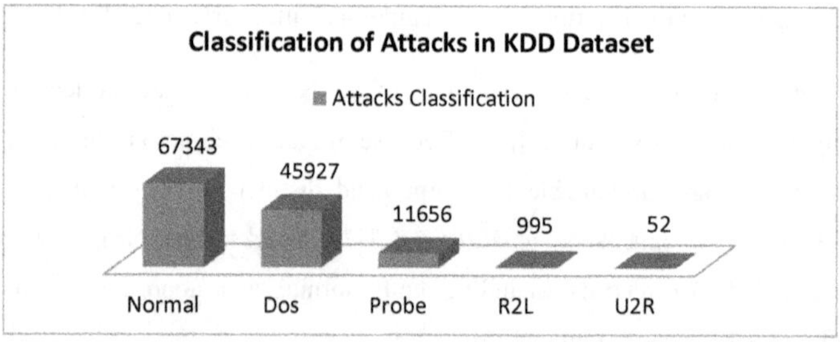

Figure 3.4: KDD Dataset Classification of Attacks

Figure 3.4 displays the quantity of all possible assaults from the KDD-Cup dataset. The analysis is finished without the use of any classifications of attack kinds. Four distinct attack types are included in this data collection, in addition to one typical type. Utilizing the given NSL_KDD data collection, a study is conducted to evaluate the resilience of the proposed framework. [29][30].

Probe: Whenever an attacker accesses information within the target network by using host and network monitoring techniques. One type of probe is port scanning.

DoS: Anytime a hacker stops prohibited users from accessing a service [31].

U2R: Anytime An individual who hacks tries to gain root access by converting a restricted user's privileges (after malware infection or stolen data) [32].

R2L: mimicking the behavior of others in the vicinity, someone else can establish wireless connection to a targeted system. R2L and U2R attacks were among the hardest to identify since they mimic the actions of normal users.

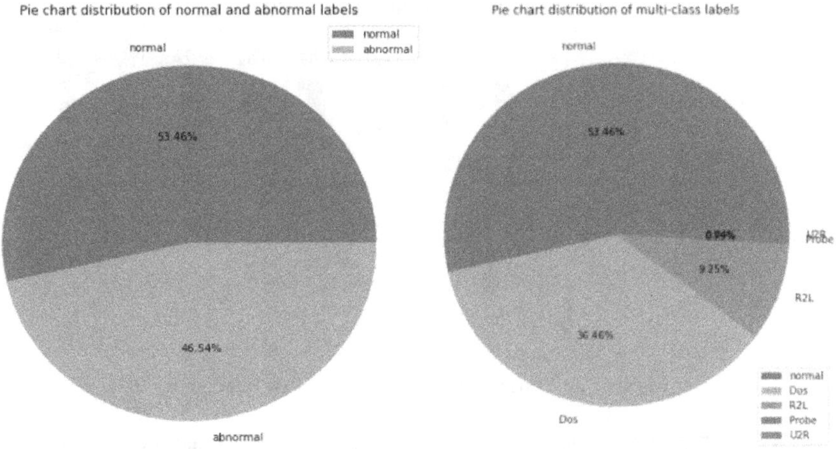

(a). Distribution of normal and abnormal labels (b) Multiclass labels distribution

Figure 3.5: NSL_KDD Dataset Analysis of Major Attacks

The distribution of attack types obtained from the KDD-Cup dataset is displayed in Figure 3.5. Figure 3.5(a) illustrates how labels are classified as abnormal or normal. Normal and unusual attacks make up 53.46% and 46.54% of all attacks, respectively. On the other hand, Figure 3.5 (b) illustrates the classification of multiclass labels, with Probe and U2R at 84%, R2L at 9.25%, DoS at 36.46%, and normal remaining at 53.46%.

Training and testing sessions covered the following five classifications: probe, normal, dos, R2L, and U2R. In this case, the lack of anomalies is indicated by the normal class. All five of these classes are taken into consideration because the results are influenced by the previous classes. With sufficient instances for every category to yield more valuable findings, these classifications are still helpful for detecting intrusions and are still reasonably imbalanced, which is an important feature of intrusion data. A set of attributes and the corresponding factors are also included; Figure 3.6 displays the datasets that depends most superior ordering distribution. The ranking is based on the coefficient of correlation, which determines the main indicators of attack kinds in the dataset.

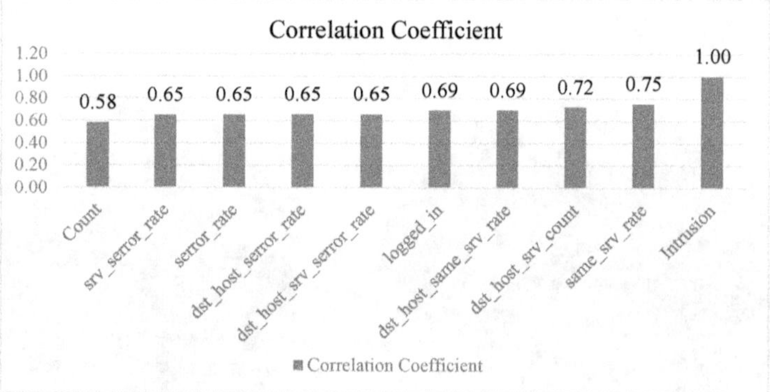

Figure 3.6: Ordering Distributions of Most Dependent Attributes

Figure 3.7 depicts the epoch vs accuracy graph for the train and test datasets constructed with 10 epochs, 500 batch sizes, and 50 neurons. The split of training and test sets, as well as the number of epochs, are used to calculate accuracy. The assessment uses 500 batches over 500 epochs and a range of neurons, as shown in Table 3.3 and Table 3.4 for bipolar and multi-classification. Four parameters are used at each epoch: correctness, average loss, precision, recall and F1 score, then we compare their values with then exclusive of CSA. Following each epoch's analysis, the average loss, we found was much lower with CSA than without; nonetheless, accuracy, precision, F1 score, and average loss, and recall, were significantly higher with CSA than without.

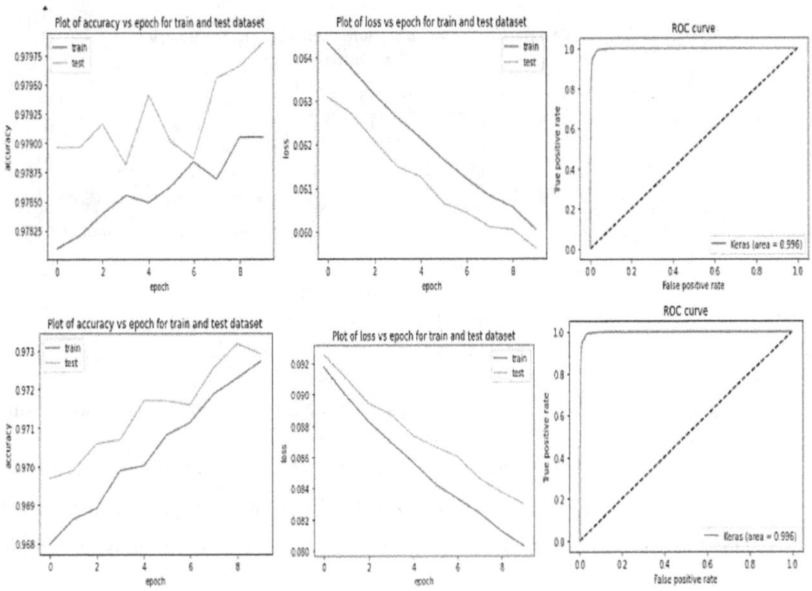

Figure 3.7: Graph of Accuracy vs Epoch

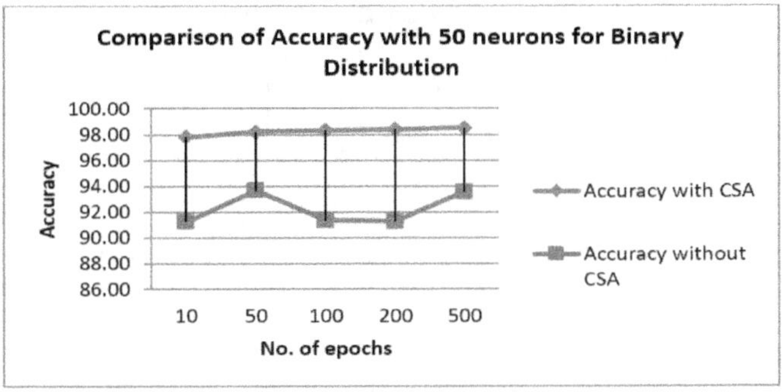

Figure 3.8: Accuracy Comparisons of 50 Neurons with Binary Distribution

Figure 3.8 depicts our work's binary distribution analysis and comparison on 50 neurons, as well as its correctness across different classification of the dataset into epochs. The charts demonstrate the efficacy of recognizing intrusions in neural network-based models with a binary set for 50 neurons produced via crow search optimization.

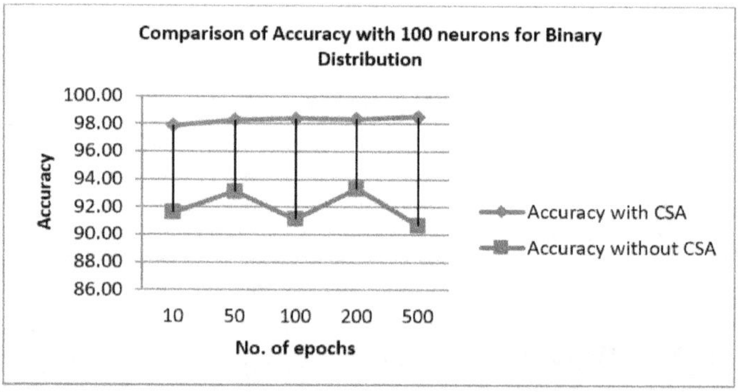

Figure 3.9: Accuracy Comparisons of 100 Neurons with Binary Distribution

Figure 3.9 depicts our work's analysis and comparison, as well as its validity for numerous epochs, by classifying the dataset's binary distribution. In identifying incursions as binaries sets, the diagrams demonstrate how well models based on neural networks employ CSO across 100 neuron layers.

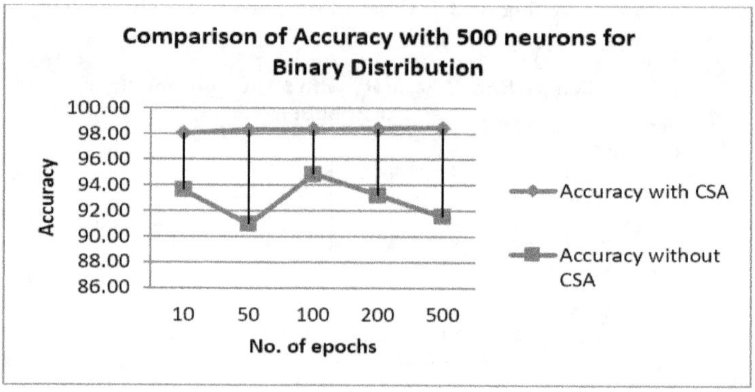

Figure 3.10: Accuracy Comparisons of 500 Neurons with Binary Distribution

Figure 3.10 compares and analyzes our work's correctness through categorizing the dataset's binary dispersal throughout different epochs. The charts display the intrusion detection rate achieved using a binary set produced by 500 neural layers using crow search optimization

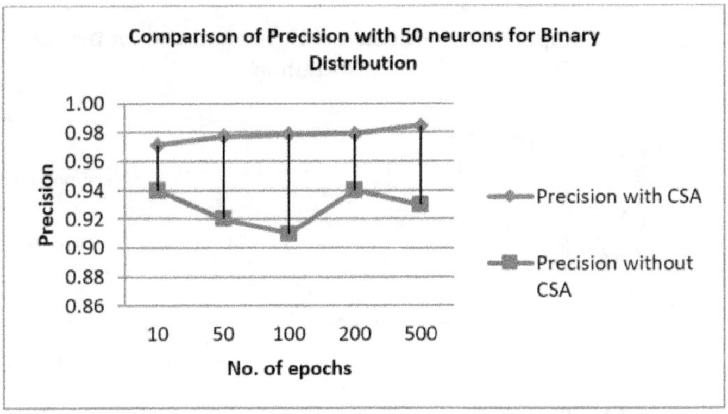

Figure 3.11: Precision Comparisons of 50 Neurons with Binary Distribution

Figure 3.11 depicts the study and contrast of our recommended study as regards of accuracy across several intervals whereas categorizing the binary distribution of the dataset. The graphs depict the performance of identifying intrusions as a binary determined by a neural network-based optimization model with 50 neural layers that use crow search optimization.

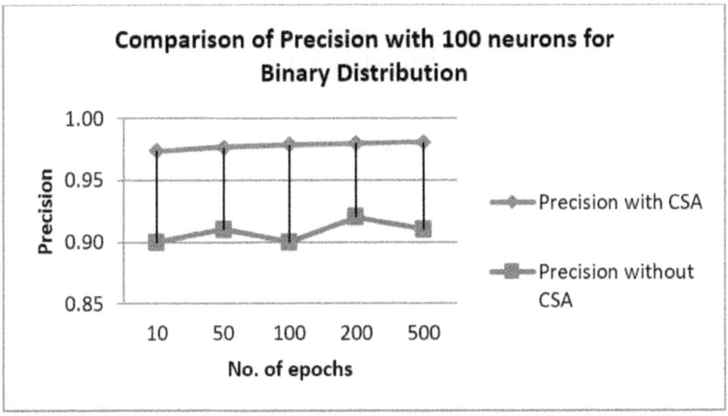

Figure 3.12: Precision Comparisons of 100 Neurons with Binary Distribution

Figure 3.12 displays the dataset's precision of binary distribution over different time periods. The images demonstrate how to use a binary dataset created by improving neural network models with 100 neuron layers to identify intrusions using CSO.

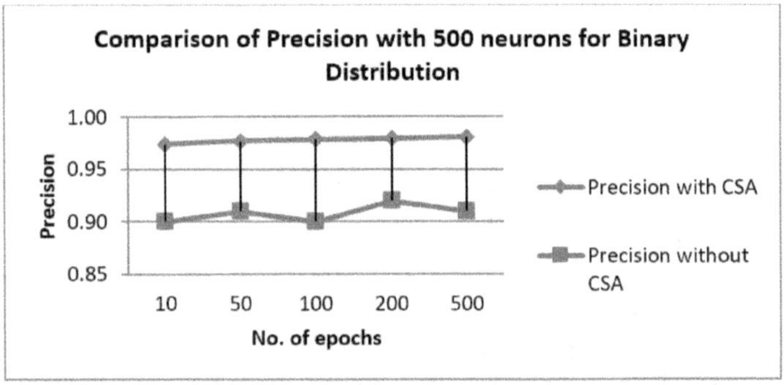

Figure 3.13: Precision Comparisons of 500 Neurons with Binary Distribution

Figure 3.13 depicts the examination and comparison with the suggested work with respect to accuracy across time periods by classifying the binary distribution of the dataset. The graphics show how well a neural network model for optimization using 500 neuron layers and crowd search engine optimization performs when detecting incursions within a binary set.

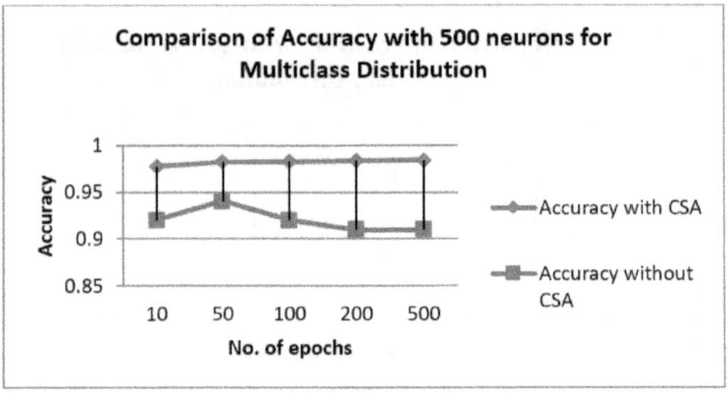

Figure 3.14: Accuracy Comparisons of 500 Neurons for Multiclass Distribution

The dataset's multiclass distributions are depicted in Figure 3.14, which also assesses the correctness of our suggested method over several time periods. The data representations illustrate the effectiveness of a multiple-class augmentation for 500 neuron stages in neural network frameworks with respect to theft detection.

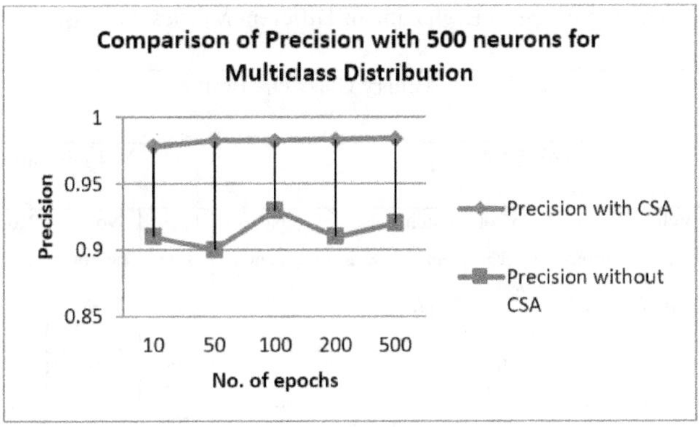

Figure 3.15: Precision Comparisons of 500 Neurons for Multiclass Distribution

Figure 3.15 depicts the multiple-class distribution of the data set being examined, as well as the evaluation and contrast of the results obtained in Precision across several epochs. The plots show how well a multiple-class collection of adjustments for 500 layers of neurons in models using NN can identify intrusions.

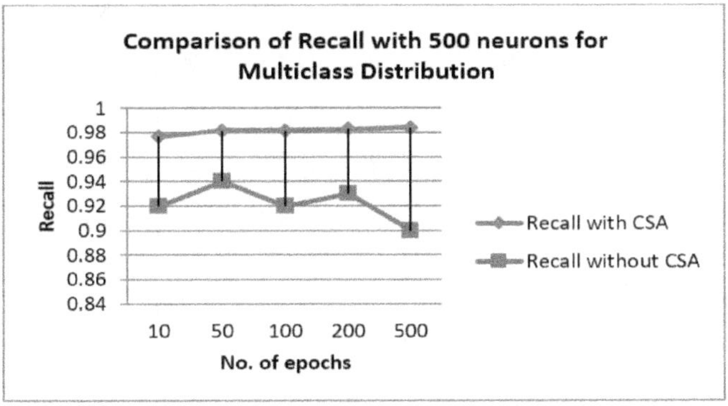

Figure 3.16: Recall Comparisons of 500 Neurons with Multiclass Distribution

The evaluation and contrast of our proposed work upon recollection for various intervals utilizing the multiclass distribution of the collected data is shown in Figure 3.16. In neural network-based models, the graphs show how effective it is to identify intrusions using a multi-class collection of improvements over 500 neuronal stages.

Table 3.3: The Performance Evaluation of Different Metrics using Binary Class Distribution

Binary Class Distribution											
NN with CSA						NN without CSA					
No. of epochs	batch size	No. of neurons	No. of epochs	batch size	No. of neurons	No. of epochs	batch size	No. of neurons	No. of epochs	batch size	No. of neurons
10	500	50	10	500	50	10	500	50	10	500	50
50	500	50	50	500	50	50	500	50	50	500	50
100	500	50	100	500	50	100	500	50	100	500	50
200	500	50	200	500	50	200	500	50	200	500	50
500	500	50	500	500	50	500	500	50	500	500	50
10	500	100	10	500	100	10	500	100	10	500	100
50	500	100	50	500	100	50	500	100	50	500	100
100	500	100	100	500	100	100	500	100	100	500	100
200	500	100	200	500	100	200	500	100	200	500	100
500	500	100	500	500	100	500	500	100	500	500	100
10	500	500	10	500	500	10	500	500	10	500	500
50	500	500	50	500	500	50	500	500	50	500	500
100	500	500	100	500	500	100	500	500	100	500	500
200	500	500	200	500	500	200	500	500	200	500	500
500	500	500	500	500	500	500	500	500	500	500	500

Table 3.3 displays the performance evaluation of different metrics using binary class distribution and compares the performance of several indicators on neural systems both with

and without CSA for binary class distribution across neuron of different sizes. It suggests that by decreasing incorrect classifications and enhancing the model's capacity to discriminate among normal and attack categories, also, the rise in a number of measures shows that CSA improves the stability of the model in managing unbalanced data.

Table 3.4: Performance Evaluation of Various Metrics in Multiclass Distribution

Multi Class Distribution												
No. of neurons	No. of epochs	batch size	NN with CSA					NN without CSA				
			Average Loss	Accuracy	Precision	Recall	F1 Score	Average Loss	Accuracy	Precision	Recall	F1 Score
50	10	500	0.08	0.97	0.97	0.97	0.97	0.57	0.92	0.9	0.91	0.91
50	50	500	0.06	0.98	0.98	0.98	0.98	0.19	0.94	0.92	0.9	0.9
50	100	500	0.06	0.98	0.98	0.98	0.98	0.37	0.92	0.94	0.92	0.92
50	200	500	0.06	0.98	0.98	0.98	0.98	0.12	0.91	0.9	0.92	0.93
50	500	500	0.06	0.98	0.98	0.98	0.98	0.37	0.91	0.93	0.9	0.9
100	10	500	0.08	0.97	0.98	0.97	0.97	0.46	0.93	0.91	0.92	0.91
100	50	500	0.06	0.98	0.98	0.98	0.98	0.51	0.9	0.94	0.92	0.9
100	100	500	0.06	0.98	0.98	0.98	0.98	0.32	0.91	0.93	0.94	0.93
100	200	500	0.06	0.98	0.98	0.98	0.98	0.38	0.91	0.91	0.93	0.91
100	500	500	0.07	0.98	0.98	0.98	0.98	0.14	0.94	0.94	0.92	0.94
500	10	500	0.07	0.98	0.98	0.98	0.98	0.36	0.93	0.91	0.92	0.93
500	50	500	0.06	0.98	0.98	0.98	0.98	0.48	0.94	0.9	0.94	0.92
500	100	500	0.06	0.98	0.98	0.98	0.98	0.14	0.93	0.93	0.92	0.91
500	200	500	0.06	0.98	0.98	0.98	0.98	0.33	0.93	0.91	0.93	0.92
500	500	500	0.07	0.98	0.98	0.98	0.98	0.59	0.91	0.92	0.9	0.93

Table 3.4 shows the results of applying NN with and without CSA to evaluate various factors on multiple-class distributions with neurons of varying sizes. All things considered, the analysis confirms that CSA helps to maximize neural network training for malware identification tasks.

Table 3.5: Evaluation of Classification Accuracy

Method	No of neurons	Accuracy
CSO-ANFIS [1] (previous-work)	-	95.80%
KNN with Inference function [7]	-	97.605%
FFNN [121] (previous-work)	10 neurons	97.97%
	20 neurons	97.16%
ANN [122](previous-work)	35 neurons	97%
HCSAOANN (NN with CSA) (proposed work)	50 neurons	98%
	100 neurons	98%
	500 neurons	98%

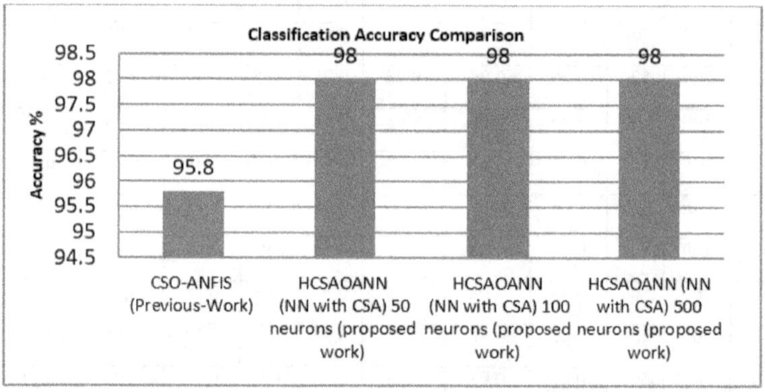

Figure 3.17: Accuracy Plot for Multiclass Distribution using 50/100/500 Neurons

Considering our accurate detection accuracy is 98%, as stated in Table 3.5, and 2.2% better than the CSO-ANFIS method, as seen in Figure 3.17, the outcomes of detection of infiltration utilizing the data set provided by NSL_KDD are superior and more effective than the prior method. Additionally, the accuracy, recall, and F1 scores attained up to 98% precision, indicating the effectiveness of the technique that was described.

Given that Table 3.5 shows that its identification rate is 98%, and 2.2% higher than the CSO-ANFIS methodology, as illustrated in Figure 3.16, the attack identification system's result compared to the prior approach, using the NSL_KDD dataset is better and greater in effectiveness. Furthermore, the effectiveness of this recommended approach was demonstrated by the precision, recall, and F1 score all reaching up to 98% accuracy.

To assist in eliminating features from complex and superfluous datasets, we offer a hybrid approach that blends a crow search optimization technique with a neural network-augmented crow search algorithm, which is also referred to as a feature selecting method. HCSAOANN is the name of the developed hybrid crow search analysis and optimization algorithm with neural network. When utilized in isolation, these overall algorithms performed better than any of its separate parts. To verify the efficacy and dependability of the HCSAOANN algorithm, information from the NSL_KDD repository were used for testing and validation. According to specific requirements, by comparing the HCSAOANN method with many popular approaches to optimization (CSA-CSO and ANN), the algorithm's efficiency was assessed, considering the number and features employed and the accuracy of the classifier's result. Comparison testing and assessments show that the proposed HCSAOANN technique performs extraordinarily well with respect to of general accuracy in classification on that data set. The proposed model outperformed earlier methods with a 98% accuracy and 98% precision rate and a low FAR of 0.45, demonstrating superior detection capability and robustness with minimal false alarms.

3.8 Summary

In summary, the results show that the HCSAOANN can outperform other algorithms after competition. The suggested HCSAOANN choice of features technique has significant applications. Data research, engineering, analysis of sentiment, and other fields can all benefit from the HCSAOANN. Enhancing this approach might lead to the implementation of an additional selection strategy to identify the most unlikely characteristics that might be the focus of further study. In the future, real-world problems like Analysis of sentiment could be studied with HCSAOANN. HCSAOANN may be tested on a variety of dataset sources.

CHAPTER - 4

ENHANCED INTRUSION DETECTION SYSTEM BASED ON RANDOM FOREST AND CROW SEARCH ALGORITHM

The intrusion detection system networking activity displays unexpected behavior due to the massive processing power. Analyzing the wide range of features becomes essential as the system gets more complex. However, features with noisy data or unsuitable features have a major impact on the effectiveness of such IDSs. The random forest method is used in this work to carry out Feature Selection (FS) to remove the meaningless quality. It increases the basic assignment of intrusion detection's efficacy with efficiency. A range of classifiers, such as recurrent neural networks, NB trees, J48, random trees, random forests, support vector machines, and Naïve Bayes multilayer perception, are then used to measure the various IDS measures. With respect to the earlier released state-of-the-art classification algorithms, the selected characteristics of the NSL_KDD dataset were passed on to the particle swarm optimization (PSO) approach, significantly reduced the false alarm rate and increased the accuracy and detection rate of the IDS. The performance indicators for the IDSs employed in this study were accuracy, precision, detection rate, and false-positive rate (FAR). To evaluate a categorization model's the efficiency for different attack groups both before and after using the CSO technique, we constructed a confusion matrix over several attack types regarding attack class and predicted class. Additionally, after using the CSO approach, we compute the Recall and Detection Rate (Alternatively referred to as True Positive Rate (TPR) or Sensitivity), and this notably assesses the preciseness of a model employing classification without CSO. This study evaluates the performance matrix component with regard to of all algorithms in addition to the proposed model. It provides outstanding accuracy with 86.92% for multiclass distribution and 88.48% for binary distribution.

4.1 Introduction

By monitoring hostile behavior and issuing alerts, computerized intrusion detection systems have developed into a powerful tool for identifying suspicious attacks. Unpredictable network traffic is a result of the intrusions and the nonlinear nature of the system [1][36].

Because of attacks and/or intrusions such as analysis of traffic, phishing, computer hacking, and other detrimental flaws, the basic security principles of confidentiality, integrity, and availability are violated, necessitating the need of IDS [37]. IDS come into two primary groups: anomaly-based IDSs and signature-based IDSs [38]. The signature-based approach is also known as misuse-based detection [59].When an association is found, this approach notifies the user and assesses the signature of the identified bogus activity. As a result, these systems have a low percentage of false alarms and may identify possible threats [39][69]. Anomaly-based systems can ward off zero-day attacks. The procedure keeps track of the frameworks' patterns and notifies the user whenever one of them diverges from the norm. The method's False-Positive Rate (FPR) is noteworthy [40][41]. IDS can be additionally separated into components that are HIDS and NIDS [57][74].

In contrast, the HIDS monitors each distinct host and generates alerts in response to system calls, application logs, log file entries, and other local hosting operations. The more features there are, the more complex the structure becomes. Because of this, the vast volume of data makes it challenging for the IDS to examine. Selecting the most important and suitable components for information security is key for spotting breaches [72]. To generate an acceptable and successful ID, it is crucial to identify important characteristics prior to pre-processing. Numerous ostentatious, irrelevant, and pertinent components are expressed in the dataset, making it more difficult to evaluate incursion and select useful features [9][41][42]. FS main goal is to improve the predictor's quality and efficacy. The current study proposes the optimal feature selection [54][55], to increase the effectiveness of intrusion detection systems with minimal computing complexity due to a collection of a few condensed features. Consequently, during the pre-processing phase, FS is used to decrease superfluous features and increase classifier efficiency. Feature selection is performed using the dataset supplied by NSL_KDD [47], an altered version that makes use of the dataset from KDD Cup 99 [12]. By using fewer features, the proposed method reduces the false alarms while improving attack identification performance. The NSL_KDD dataset contains 125973 records including both normal and attack nodes, despite its usefulness, it is not up to date with new threats and contemporary network traffic. [76]. Studies on every data point are made feasible by its lower, easier-to-manage size. The goal of this study is to maximize the algorithm's accuracy using the application of crow search optimization [71][72].

4.2 Purpose of Study

The necessity to focus on the challenges and issues related to IDS in the broader context of safeguarding networks is what spurred the inquiry. The following are the main reasons for the research:

- Unpredictable Network Traffic Behavior: The necessity to develop more adaptable and robust IDS which may handle the unpredictability of modern network activity is what motivates this research.
- Complexity and Irrelevance of Features: The distortion and complexities brought on by the vast number of characteristics required by IDS affect the efficiency of the system. Finding and focusing on relevant qualities whereas excluding things that don't matter is essential to accelerating the identification procedure and improving the preciseness of the entire system. The investigation has been inspired by this matter.
- Effects in the Realistic Application: Improving intrusion detection systems practicality and usefulness in real-world scenarios is the primary objective. By addressing significant problems and enhancing IDS performance indicators, the goal of this study is to improve the current state of online safety [45], and ultimately contribute to the creation of safeguards for networks that are more adaptable and robust.

4.3 NSL_KDD Dataset's Overview

The KDD Cup 99 collection has been changed to become the dataset maintained by the NSL_KDD [58]. The dataset, include 4 types of attacks are described below, that has 41 attributes that are categorized into five classes: two standard classes and four assault categories. The 42 characteristics, the class features, provide further details about these kinds.

- **U2R (User to Root):** U2R describes the locations where an outsider exploits the vulnerabilities in local computers, including rootkits, SQL attacks, and spy software, to get access.

- **DoS (Denial of Service):** DoS attacks are those that prevent authorized users from using a system; examples include SYN Smurf, teardrop, floods, and Neptune.
- **Probe:** The idea of a probing attack includes the situation in which an intruder analyses network traffic to discover more about the operations of the network. These include Satan, ping-sweep, Nmap, and port-scan.
- **R2L (Root to Local):** Malware like Warez Master, Imap, Spy, and Multihope that attempt to gain illegal access to a remote system satisfy the R2L standards for a breach.

The features of each dataset now have four labels [46]:

- **Domain knowledge:** These are the traits that are present in the linkages. This label is associated with 13 properties.
- **Basic:** As is customary, each of these attributes has a transmission control protocol, or TCP, association. This term is associated with nine features.
- **Host:** Information about the host group can be used to determine whether an attack has the capacity to last more than two seconds. That category includes ten features.
- **Traffic:** The attributes described using 2-S windows fall under this category. This categorization encompasses nine characteristics.

The graphical representation of attack frequencies in Figure 4.1, the dataset generated by the NSL_KDD is displayed. The statistical information for the KDD Cup 99 datasets and the NSL_KDD datasets are shown in Figure 4.2 and Figure 4.3. To separate the training and testing sets' results, four distinct assault kinds are used. The one which was employed for the training set has 22 different types of hits, whereas the one used for the test set has 17 extra attacks [46][47][48]. Dataset acts as a standard against which individuals may evaluate the effectiveness of various IDS methods include both positive and negative examples. Because there are no duplicates of information in the learning set, predictive models are not skewed against frequently occurring data items. Across the testing set as well as the training set due to a significant amount of redundant entries in the initial version of KDD '99, analyzers were skewed towards frequently occurring connection classes. Plenty of such were eliminated by NSL_KDD to create an enhanced equal representation.

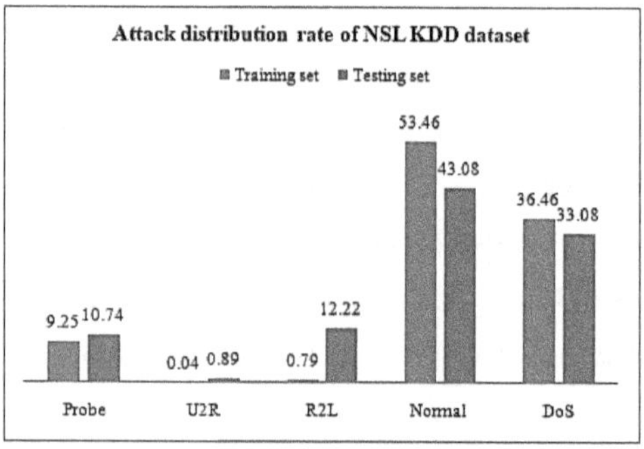

Figure 4.1: Attack Distribution Frequencies (NSL_KDD Dataset)

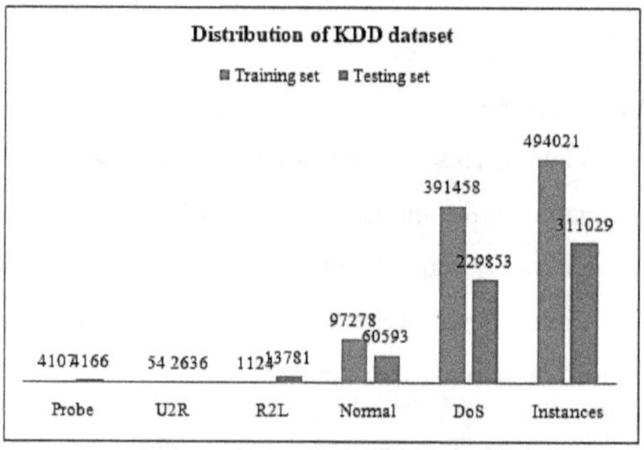

Figure 4.2: Distributions (KDD Dataset)

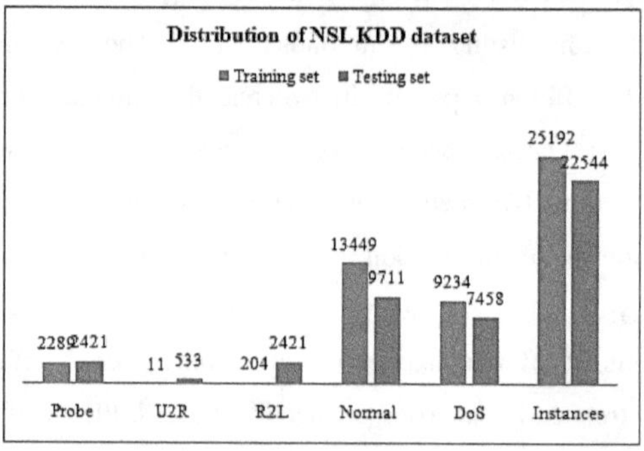

Figure 4.3: Distributions (NSL_KDD Dataset)

4.4 Artificial Intelligence Classifiers

To examine both the test and training sets, we employed the subsequent machine learning models [50] within the NSL_KDD dataset.

Naive Bayes (NB): It is usually difficult to express the probability relationship between values when they have statistical or causal correlations. Other factors may be affected by a computational parameter [62]. The probabilistic framework consists of Naive Bayesian frameworks intended to take advantage of any possible statistical or casual connection between the issue's random variables. This classification technique performs well when applied to a specific selection of attribute measurements since variables in this specific case are regarded as distinct [52].

SVM: Two separate hyper planes make up the SVM classifier, which was developed There should be a lot of space between these. This technique's basic principle is to increase the spacing between the positive and negative classifications to create a hyper plane. The critical information elements that establish the location and direction of the ideal dividing border, also known as a hyper plane, constitute support vectors. The best-separated hyper plane on SVM can be discovered in a dimension region of elements that is more important than the vector being utilized, which is transferred to a bigger dimensionality space of features [47]. SVM typically exhibits low rationalizing errors or is not affected by the issue of over fitting the training data set. A predictive model is considered to have serious over-fitting or generalized errors when it performs negatively on situations that weren't considered in its training phase. Users can select each dimension of the total number of erroneously categorized samples and decision limits using the parameter that governs the penalized ratio. It's a useful method for regressive and categorical problems. A computer-aided design, or CAD, technique was then developed to separate images into groups of two. SVM has been used by the researcher in the Alzheimer's disease (AD) and out of 126 brain MRI samples that the researchers identify 28 are Alzheimer's disease and the remaining samples were normal. In this case, the Displacement Field (DF) is employed to track the shape changes from healthy brains to brains with Alzheimer's disease. Researchers have also used the Support Vector Machine [66], and its two image classification variations, Twin SVM (TSVM) and Generalized Eigen-Value Proximal SVM (GEPSVM).

KNN: KNN also called as k-Nearest Neighbor, is a straightforward, visually appealing non-parametric statistical method for regressing and categorizing data. Determine the estimated distance between the unlabeled location determined through the KNN method and the different input vector scores [63]. The percentage of instances in the test and validation dataset's that closest resemble the given assessments is indicated by the k element. An additional point is classified using that classifier, which uses a substantial proportion of the voting obtained for the closest place in the data being trained. The Euclidean distance, which is a measure of distance between two data point, has been used to determine how similar the two data point seem.

Logistic Regression (LR): The link among the classifying variable that is dependent and the factors that are not dependent is investigated in this research, primarily focusing on binary values such as 1 or 0, no or yes. The basis for creating a probability that establishes the algorithm's outcome based on a binomial distribution is attributes [60].

Decision Tree (DT): A set of decisions is used to classify an instance within the decision tree, with the current choice influencing the subsequent choices [51]. Every leaf branch denotes a different classification group, and the dataset is categorized as its main junction all the way up to the offspring node. Each node in it stands for the sample's characteristics.

Random Forest (RF): Decision Tree, or DT, and ensemble modeling are combined in a machine learning approach known as Random Forest. The forest is made up of different trees, while the attributes are selected at random as input [73]. The approach builds a random subset of data and numerous DTs using a bagging technique. This approach is believed to have been particularly effective for almost all predicting problems. Almost every regression or classifier problem may be solved using it. The variables contained in a randomly selected vector that is uniformly distributed among all the trees within the forest serve as the basis for each tree's estimate in this arrangement of tree predictors. There were two components to the approach. To create the random forest, 'k' Random Trees is created in the first stage [65]. These DTs with same test features are combined in the following phase. The outcome prediction is made up of its most frequent DT or an assessment of each DT. Implementing the method is simple, it produces better accuracy even when information is inconsistent, and it offers an assessment of the characteristics needed for classification.

It produces an internal, impartial assessment of the total error while operating on huge dataset's. It additionally includes a technique that stabilizes variance in the distribution of the class for datasets that contain imbalances. The randomization approach primarily enables statisticians to cut down on the amount of time spent preparing the data because it requires no input processing and may evaluate numerical information and specific characteristics without transformation or scaling. The ensemble's approach, which runs many of the DTs by training them, returns the group that has the most entries out of all the trees. Random forests perform somewhat better than SVMs. To construct a forest with controlled variance, a collection of trees is put together [70]. To make its forecast, the classification algorithm employs either weighted voting or majority voting. The algorithm is depicted in a flow diagram in Figure 4.4.

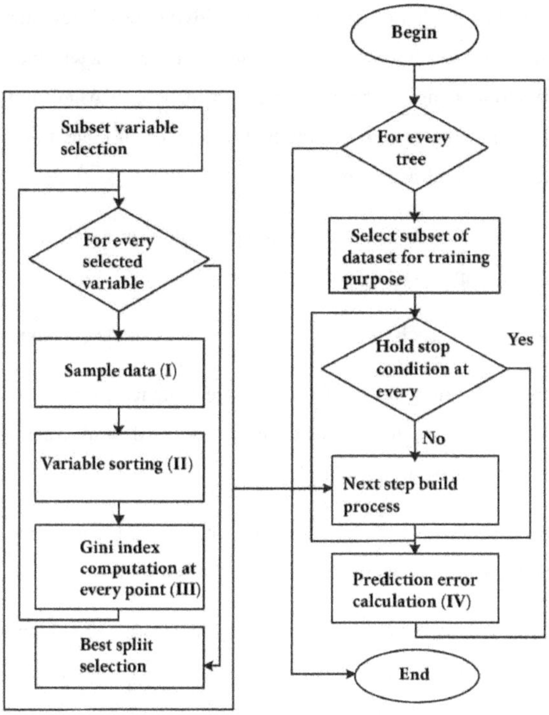

Figure 4.4: RF Flow Graph

Working of Random Forest: The jth core learners are created using tree $h_i(L, \Theta j)$, where j's is a set of unpredictability factors that separately work with $j = 1,...,J$. With $DT_r = (x_1, y_1), (x_2, y_2),.....(x_n, y_n)$ as the training data, $x_k = (x_k, 1,..........,x_k, p)$ N represents the y_k represents the result and f represent the predictors. A specific instantiation Θ_j of Θ_k, its trained trees are represented as $g_i(x, \Theta_i, DT_r)$. Even though this model depends on, the component of unpredictability, i have not been specifically considered.

Despite this, it is used to inconceivably add two randomized steps. It is used to inconceivably add two randomized steps. All of the trees in the beginning phases have incorporated a unique bootstrapping strategy using the original data sets that additionally make use of bagging. The bootstrap sample creates a single part of j by randomizing the data. The optimal divide is determined by examining a fraction of every one of the g components used as predictors, rather than employing all of predictors during the randomly selected stage of the second stage. Randomness is used to determine the remaining part of j using the prediction sample. The random forest, or RF, in Algorithm 4.1, pseudo-coding is displayed. As mentioned earlier, this method makes use of many trees, every one that is built using the procedures outlined below:

1. Assumptions: A and B are the training samples, respectively, and the technique for machine learning employs a few parameters [61].

2. To find the result for each tree vertex, we need b parameters as inputs and $b < B$.

3. Bootstrapping sampling or selecting a single instance to replicate it from every trainee event are the methods used in this tree to select a set of data for training. The error of the tree is estimated using the remaining samples.

4. A random selection of b parameters has been made at each node in the tree. The ideal split of a training dataset is determined by those b parameters.

5. All the trees are fully grown and have not been sheared. One item of data is projected by moving it down a tree. A training dataset is labeled at the node's end terminal. After a last iteration of the whole set of trees, RF's prediction is expressed by figuring out each tree's median voting.

Among the advantages of this approach are the following:

1. Suitable for both regression and classification issues.
2. Classifiers for categories are naturally managed.
3. Regardless of serious problems, fitting is simple and quick to operate.
4. Non-parametric distributional constraints are not stated explicitly.
5. It can manage very erratic connectivity and classification constraints.
6. Automated variable selection.
7. Uses proximity as a stand-in parameter to manage missing data.
8. Outlier identification, outlier visualization, and unsupervised learning.

Algorithm 4.1: Random Forest Method

Let $x_k = (x_k,1, \ldots\ldots, x_p)^N$ and $DT_r = (x_1, y_1)\ldots\ldots\ldots (x_n, y_n)$ represent the training data.

2. If j is equal to J, do

3. Create DT_r using the bootstrapping sequence D_j of size n.

4. Using data for training from the bootstrapping sequence D_j, binary partitioning that recursively fits a tree.

5. Begin every observation in a different node.

6. Perform step 7. Repeat step (i) for each un-split node. Out of the f viable predictors, choose the g predictors at random (ii). Find the best binary division among all the divisions into binary employing the g predictors from step 1.

7. Divide a node among two children's nodes using the divisions from step 2.

8. Until termination requirements are met;

9. End

10. End

11. To anticipate everything at a subsequent stage, use the regression formula.

$$F(x) = \frac{1}{J}\sum_{J=1}^{J} g_i(x) \quad (4.1)$$

For classification, use

$$f(x) = \arg\max b \frac{1}{J}\sum_{J=1}^{J} I(g_l(x) = y) \quad (4.2)$$

Therefore, the anticipated outcome of the counter elements at x is represented by g using a lth tree. The Eq, 4.1 and Eq. 4.2 shows the regression and classification.

4.5 Swarm Intelligence

A population-based, organically influenced approach, swarm intelligence may tackle difficult problems and provide dependable, efficient, and affordable solutions [63]. It's a subfield of artificial intelligence that studies how termites or insects, honeybees, ants, and bird flocks behave. They have limited social interaction skills and rely on specific behavioral features to establish rudimentary connections to survive. The main form of interaction is either verbal or visual, such as watching the bees dance and flutter. Observe how a substance alters the environment and other entities. For example, ants create pheromone trails as they move around, searching for indirect communication between agents. Swarm intelligence is applied to scheduling, machine learning [69], data analysis, medical informatics, bioinformatics, operations research, and the resolution of commercial and financial problems. Swarm intelligence was simply defined as the common practice of fundamental or basic intelligence within social agents [64]. The swarm intelligence approach uses the following criteria to find a group of responses:

Alternative Response Theory: solutions are not limited by channels.

Consistency idea: According to this idea, actions remain constant in a variety of situations.

Adaptability Principle: The adaptation principle is the capacity to adapt to novel situations through effective time- and space-based computations.

The same idea underlies appropriate computing for the successful implementation of space-related and time-sensitive solutions. One of the most important quality principles is the incorporation of environmental high-quality elements.

4.6 The PSO Approach

Based on the behaviour of bird flocks, the PSO, sometimes called the particle swarm optimisation method, has uses in many different scientific disciplines.

It involves adjusting to social animals whose relationships and movements are continuously changing, like fish and birds. Depending on the specified searching region, a swarm of particles having randomly beginning positions and velocities is first generated at arbitrary. The workflow graph parameters for the PSO approach are shown in Figure 4.5. Both experiences and knowledge gained through teamwork are integrated into the PSO's algorithm. Birds' propensity to congregate aids in achieving the best results. The birds follow a predetermined path to find their targeted food sources [67]. This path, also known as the personal best (particle's best) solution, is believed to be the most effective one [49].

Each particle explores the search area for the optimal result while evaluating its unique floating experience and the experiences of the other particles in the community. An additional most outstanding value for fitness is obtained by keeping an eye on the particle of each group in close proximity to the other particle's region [64]. It's said to be the best. Each particle has a speed that matches the velocity required to get to the best. Finding an overall optimal solution is the aim of PSO, which entails guiding. All particles move in the direction of pbest and gbest at each stage using movable weights. This method provides for better explorations and extractions [68]. The PSO algorithm's equation is written as

$$s_{id}(t+1) = s_{id}(t) + m_1 N_1 (p_{id}(t) - z_{id}(t)) + m_2 N_2 (p_{gd}(t) - z_{id}(t)) \qquad (4.3)$$

$$z_{id}(t+1) = z_{id}(t) + s_{id}(t+1) \qquad (4.4)$$

In the dth element, $s_{id}(t)$ signifys the velocity of the ith particle at the tth iteration. The tth iteration's acceleration factors are m_1 and m_2, respectively, in terms of societal and personal awareness. $Z_{id}(t)$ is a representation of an ith particle's location at the tth recurrence d^{th} dimension. pgd(t) represents the position reached as the total population up until the tth iteration, while $p_{kd}(t)$ represents the pbest position occupied by the ith particles in the dth dimension during the tth iteration; N_1 and N_2 are two arbitrary values ranging from 0 to 1 in order to avoid premature convergence.

4.7 Proposed Methodology

The proposed approach is based on the hybrid combination of random forest and crow search optimization. The basic steps of implemented model are as follows:

4.7.1 Preliminary Processing

False alerts were caused by the classifiers simple characteristics. As a result, it is crucial to preprocess the dataset. Furthermore, the classification approaches are unable to overcome the increased computing time and storage requirements caused by some common traits. The NSL_KDD dataset's estimated characteristics are shown as:

$$FS = \{cs_1, cs_2, cs_3, cs_4, \ldots\ldots\ldots\ldots cs_n\}$$

FS, signifying the collection's n properties. Common traits are eliminated out of basic features due to the cost and repetition. Roughly modified elements are displayed as

$$FS' = \{cs_1, cs_2, cs_3, cs_4, \ldots\ldots\ldots\ldots cs_p\}$$

The number p represents the rough features that remain after removal. Furthermore, additional preprocessing is needed to generate the ideal selection of elements based on the dataset's relevance. The significance of feature transformation and reduction in features is explained in the upcoming section that follows [71].

4.7.2 The FS Method

In this section, we suggest the FS technique using a mathematical equation. FS is represented by six tuples: $FS = \{D, F, T, S, T_s, E_m\}$, where $D = \{x_1, x_2, x_3, \ldots\ldots x_i\}$, that a dataset with k instances, $F = \{f_1, f_2, f_3, \ldots\ldots f_c\}$ with c features, $T = \{t_1, t_2, t_3, \ldots.t_n\}$ by n categorization of target classes, and S is a search space, that is an illustration of the set of features F that contains every partition that can be made from F, $\{s_1, s_2, s_3, \ldots.s_m\} = S$ By sj $= \{f_u, f_v, \ldots.f_w\}$, (m = 2n - 1) Where m <= u!= v!= w <= n, Function fs represents the modification in the syntax of FS: fs: F→S, while E_m is an evaluation metric. The process of creating the ideal subset or subsets and eliminating superfluous features within the datasets is known as FS [67]. By selecting a specific portion of a feature, this method seeks to increase forecast performance while streamlining efficiency and computation. The procedures that were followed in FS are depicted and explained in Figure 4.5. By concentrating on the majority of instructive data, it prevents problems like inaccurate fitting and the affliction of dimensions, streamlines algorithms, and cuts down on time spent on training.

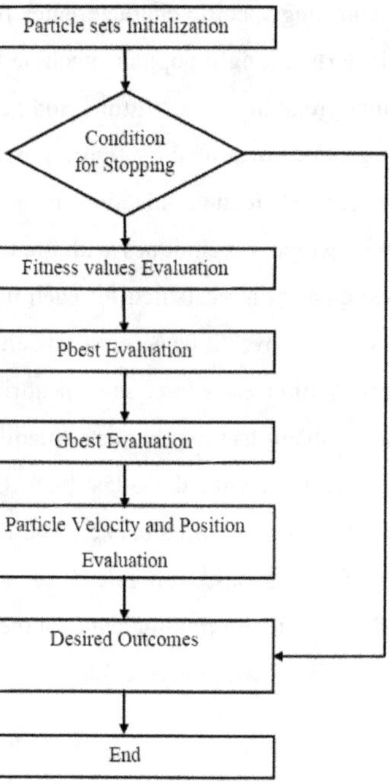

Figure 4.5: The PSO System

1. The estimating modules assess the suitability of the subsets by using several measurement factors.

2. The later descendants from the original features package are triggered by the generating method.

3. The validity of the feature subset is checked by a validation function.

4. The ideal subset of the feature is determined at this point.

4.8 Proposed Work

Pre-processing of dataset is used in this research to choose the properties features. When necessary due to the persistence of inaccurate and superfluous characteristics in the dataset, FS is the technique of choosing specific characteristics from the initial data source. The RF method is among particularly strongly popular machine learning methods for FS. Excellent prediction, decreased interpretability, over-fitting, and performance are all displayed by this approach. Understanding is demonstrated by figuring out the importance of each parameter in relation to DT. The term RF feature selection using integrated techniques is frequently used. This method blends wrapper techniques with qualitative filters. A randomized feature taken from the complete data set is evaluated for each tree of the trees in RF. Decor-related trees are generally less prone to overfit because the specific tree does not explore the features that make up the others. Within each tree, several attribute-based yes-or-no questions are posed. Every site of the problem has two buckets established, each of which keeps track of the relationships and differences with the other bucket. That demonstrates the value and worth of every quality that shows up in its bucket. The RF classification system then selects the ten most important features based on relevance and eliminates other less important features from each of the testing and training data sources of the NSL_KDD collection. The feature selections approach is shown in Figure 4.6.

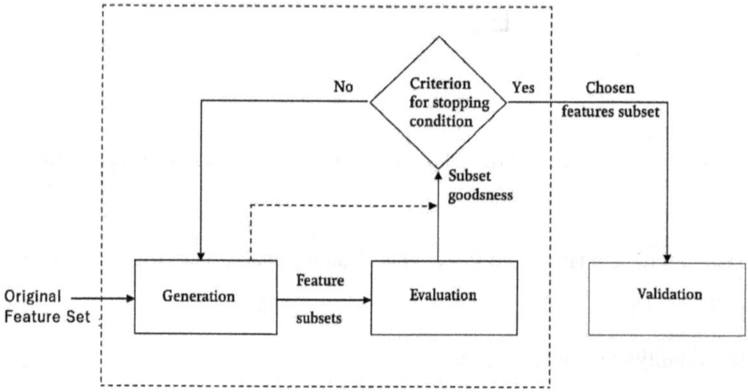

Figure 4.6: Feature Selections

The proposed PSO method was designed using Algorithm 4.2. Except for a single class feature, the training group has 41 items because the dataset's has 41 characteristics within the sets for training and for testing. Category variables are converted into a framework that machine learning algorithms can utilize to produce better estimations with the help of the one-hot encode function.

Algorithm 4.2: FS-CSO (Proposed Approach)

Input: Preprocessing whole features with the KDD dataset.

Output: Show the classifier's performance matrix, detection rate, recall, and classification results.

Function Process_model()

1. The random forest technique is utilized to apply FS on the KDD dataset. (as per Algorithm 1)

   Eliminate the attribute "difficulty_level".

2. Link attack class names to attack labels.
3. Pick numerical characteristics.
4. Use Standard Scalar for categorical properties.
5. Use one-hot encoding for properties that are categorical.

$$Z_{scaled} = (Z - \mu)/\sigma$$

Where;

Z represents the primary features.

$\boldsymbol{\sigma}$ represents the feature's standard deviation.

m represents the feature's mean.

Zscaled represents the feature standardization.

6. Analyze factors that are substantially connected (Pearson correlation > 0.5).

7. Combine certain qualities with categorical data that has been one-hot encoded.
8. Divide the dataset into training and testing (75/25%) categories.
9. Setup the parameters for the crow search.

$$z_k (t+1) = z_k (t) + X * (z_k (t) - z_j (t)) + a_1 * (z_i (t) - z_k(t)) + a_2 * (x_b (t) - x_k (t))$$

$$V_k (t+1) = a_1 * rand() * (z_j (t) - z_k (t)) + (z_i (t) - z_k (t)) * a_2 * rand() + X * V_k(t)$$

10. Repetition for max_iterations.

    a. Use the current crow positions to train the neural network model

    b. Assess the model's precision.

    c. Adjust crow locations by accuracy and optimization criteria.

11. A model that is optimized for attack classification and prediction.

End

Here, $z_k(t)$ denotes the kth crow's existing position at time t, $z_k(t + 1)$ denotes the kth crow's new position at time t + 1, $Z_i(t)$ denotes the ideal location within the crows' memories, V_k (t) denotes the kth crow's functioning velocity at time t, $V_k(t+1)$ denotes the fresh velocity of kth crow on time t+1, $x_j(t)$ denotes the ideal position within the jth crow's memory, $z_b(t)$ denotes the ideal position among all crows, X denotes the dimension of the examination step, and a_1 and a_2 denote the learning rates. Between 0 and 1, the random number is represented by rand(). When these 41 variables are hot encoded, 74 variables are produced. These features are used as a layer of input by the undetectable part of the artificially generated neural network [53], which consists of 20 neurons and is used to compute the calculation. The propagation that moves ahead is represented by a mathematical variable. These compute the neural network's forward propagation and degradation [75]. To return the proper biases and weights, it must transform a few variables that are supplied. After forward propagation, the PSO approach is applied to a small portion of the attributes of the data set employing many passes and a restricted number of particles to determine which iteration perform best. The proposed methodology is illustrated in Figure 4.7 which includes all the steps how attacks are classify into its categories.

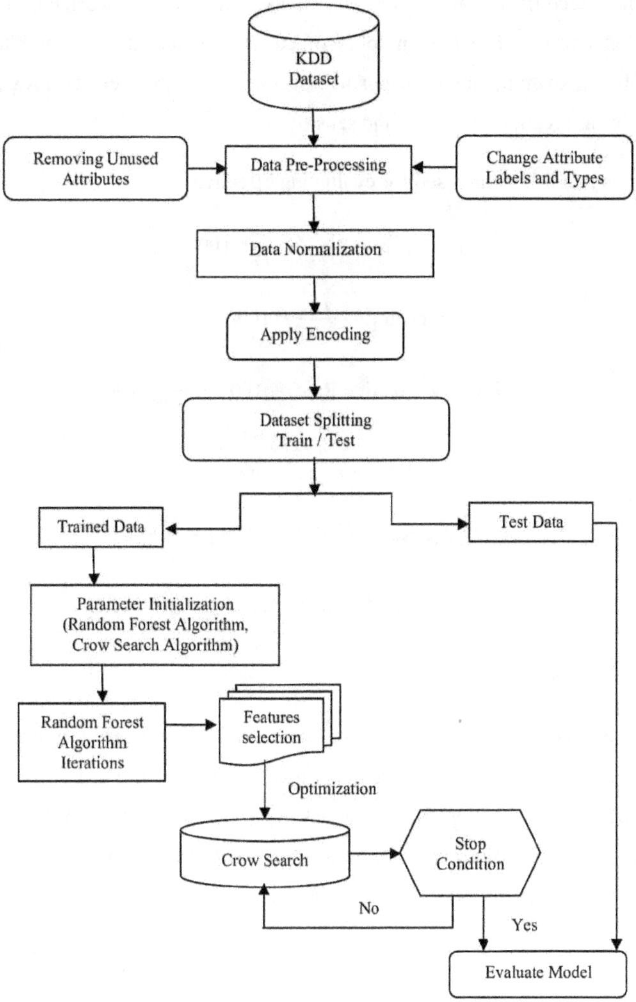

Figure 4.7: Proposed Methodologies

4.8.1 Performance Measure

To evaluate performance of the proposed framework, the FPR and TPR are computed. FAR and FPR are other terms for the classification of valid traffic. To calculate them, divide all of the normal records by all of the intrusions which were incorrectly recognized using conventional forms. The total number of correctly detected instances that were positive divided by the overall amount of positive occurrences is the Detection Rate DR. The DR is also known as recall, failure rate, and sensitivity.

The factors that follow are used for evaluating effectiveness:

$$\text{F1- Score} = 2\frac{TP}{TP+FN+FP} * 100 \quad (4.5)$$

$$\text{Precision} = \frac{TP}{TP+FP} * 100 \quad (4.6)$$

$$\text{FPR (False Positive Rate)} = 100 - \frac{TP}{TP+FN} * 100 \quad (4.7)$$

$$\text{Accuracy} = \frac{TP+TN}{TP+FP+TN+FN} \quad (4.8)$$

$$\text{FNR (False Negative Rate)} = 100 - \frac{TP}{TP+FN} * 100 \quad (4.9)$$

$$\text{TPR (True Positive Rate)} = \frac{TP}{TP+FN} * 100 \quad (4.10)$$

4.9 Results and Discussion

A confusion matrix between several sorts of assaults with regard to predicted category and offensive class allows one should consider the CSO technique while assessing the efficacy of an identification system for different attack types. For popular attack types in this scenario, including DoS, R2L, non-attack (Normal), U2R, and Probe, One conceivable configuration for our confusion matrix [76][77] is as follows:

True Positives (TP): TP are instances where the model accurately classified a fraudulent class as falling under a particular category, such as identifying a DoS assault as such. Mislabeling normal network traffic as a result of a DoS attack is one example.

False Negatives (FN): Instances when a certain attack class was mistakenly classified as a non-attack class by the model. For example, not immediately identifying a denial-of-service assault. It is similar to a safeguard keeping watch over the entrance but allowing an intruder to get past undetected.

False Positives (FP): When a non-attack class is incorrectly predicted by the model to be a specific attack class.

True Negatives (TN): Situations in which the framework has accurately identified a non-attack category. This means being able to tell whenever an offense isn't taking place.

Table 4.1: Confusion Matrix of Different Attacks without CSO

Attack Class	Predicted Class				
	Normal	Dos	U2R	R2L	Probe
Normal	9428	91	4	53	38
Dos	17	7343	0	1	1
U2R	9	0	53	7	0
R2L	198	120	2	2467	1
Probe	46	1338	0	0	942

Table 4.1 display the confusion matrix of different attacks without CSO. Using this confusion matrix, we can evaluate the model's performance for every sort of assault separately, as well as its accuracy in identifying normal network traffic. We may calculate pertinent parameters including accuracy, F1 score, and recall for all attack class to assess how well the model distinguishes between different non-attacks and assaults. Even without the use of optimization techniques like CSO, this study provides useful insights into how well the model works for specific threat classes.

Table 4.2: Confusion Matrix of Different Attacks After using CSO

Attack Class	Predicted Class				
	Normal	Dos	U2R	R2L	Probe
Normal	9611	0	1	0	2
Dos	4	7356	0	1	1
U2R	1	0	67	1	0
R2L	3	2	2	2780	1
Probe	7	10	0	0	2309

The predicted and actual attacks are shown in Table 4.2. By combining the CSO approach with a confusion matrix several advantages may be obtained including optimized attack category discrimination, reduced false negatives and positives, higher model accuracy, more effective threshold selection, universal optimization, durability to noisy data, faster convergence, customized solutions, and the potential to reduce human intervention in model tuning. The model is now more effective, efficient, and adaptable for a variety of application types because of the adjustment of CSO characteristics. This is particularly true in categorization and cyber security operations, because it is crucial to minimize false alarms and identify attacks effectively.

Table 4.3: Detection Rate and Recall Performance Classification without CSO

	Dos (%)	Probe (%)	R2L (%)	U2R (%)
Detection Rate	99.75	68.67	88.48	76.03
Recall	81.79	96.03	97.62	89.28

Table 4.4: Detection Rate and Recall Performance Classification after using CSO

	Dos (%)	Probe (%)	R2L (%)	U2R (%)
Detection Rate	99.9	97.8	99.7	97.1
Recall	98.3	98.67	99.04	97.45

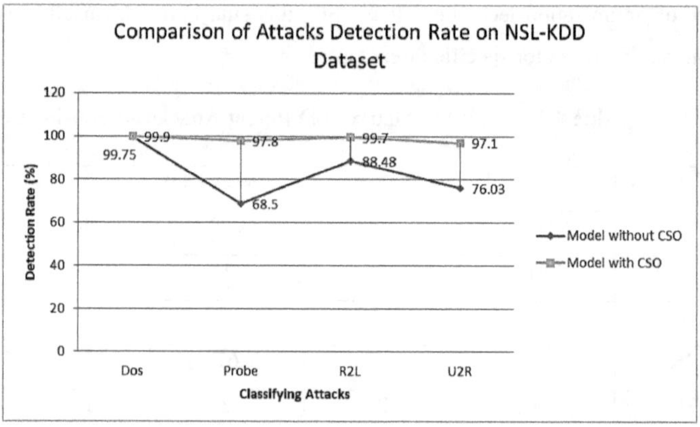

Figure 4.8: Comparison of the NSL_KDD Dataset Attack Detection Rate

Table 4.3 and Table 4.4 provide the detection rate and recall results for categories regardless of the CSO, correspondingly. It is clear that a very high detection rate is achieved when the CSO is used.

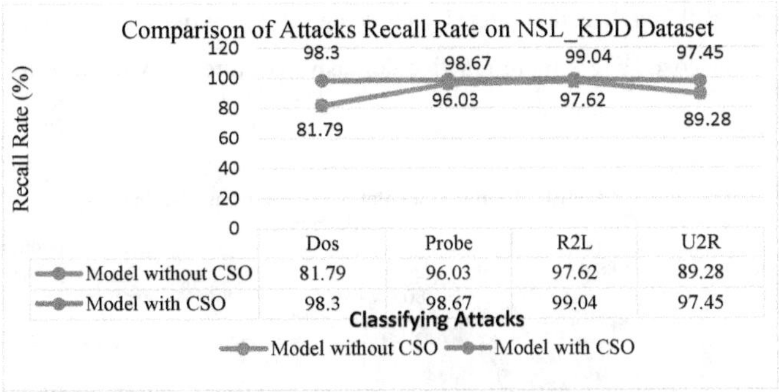

Figure 4.9: Attack Recall Rate Comparisons on the NSL_KDD Dataset

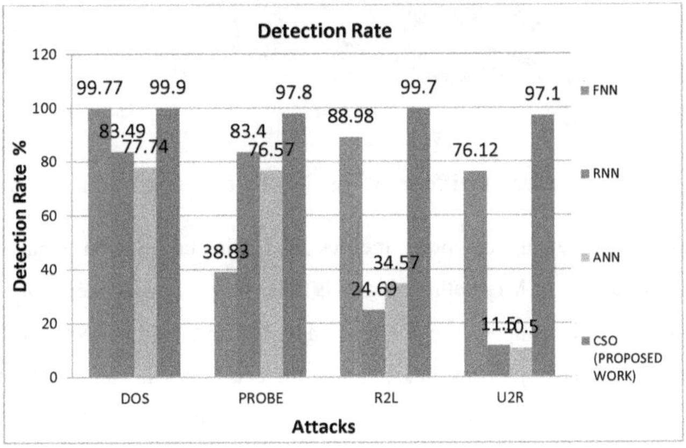

Figure 4.10: Attack Detection Rate Comparisons with Other Models

As seen in Figure 4.8 and Figure 4.9, employing the CSO to assess the recall and detection rate for certain assault categories, such as ordinary congestion, U2R, DOS, and R2L, has a number of computational advantages. CSO parameter optimization increases the model's ability to detect assaults by lowering the likelihood of false negatives. Its wide range of optimization capabilities ensures dependable performance in a variety of data distributions and situations, and its customized performance may be adjusted to suit specific requirements.

As seen in Figure 4.10, optimal threshold selection and quicker convergence also lead to enhanced recall and detection rates. By reducing false negatives, CSO can result in increased safety, lower costs, and a more reactive defensive posture in cyber security and identifying threats.

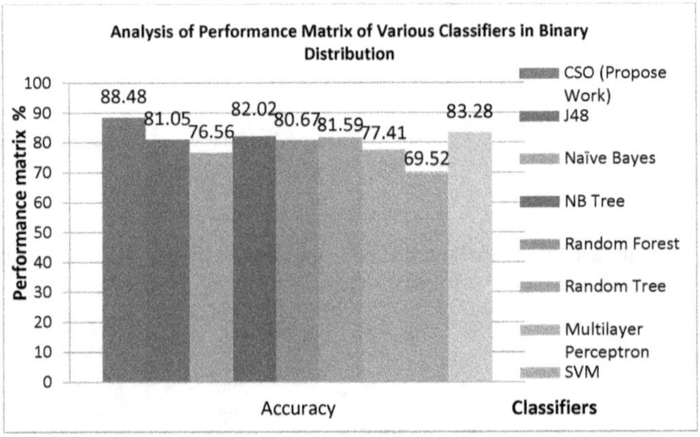

Figure 4.11: Evaluation of Different Classifiers Performance Matrix in Binary Distribution

To determine different categories metrics for efficiency within binary distributions, a thorough evaluation of ML methodologies is necessary for tasks like binary classification, as seen in Figure 4.11. Support vector machines, NB trees, J48, RNN, random forests, and naïve Bayes multilayer perceptron are among the classifiers that are taken into consideration, using a number of effectiveness criteria. These measures include the confusion matrix, F1-score, accuracy, and other parameters. The assessment technique seeks to determine which classifiers, given the particular requirements of the scenario, best combine the trade-offs between accuracy, recall, and other metrics. Hyper parameter tweaking and cross-validation techniques are commonly used to increase efficiency and guarantee accurate generalization and selection of models. Because ability significantly influences classifier selections, this investigation is crucial for figuring out the optimal approach for a binary classification issue.

In this instance, each classifier is used to assess the performance matrix variable, as the proposed approach exhibits outstanding results using an 88.48% binary distribution.

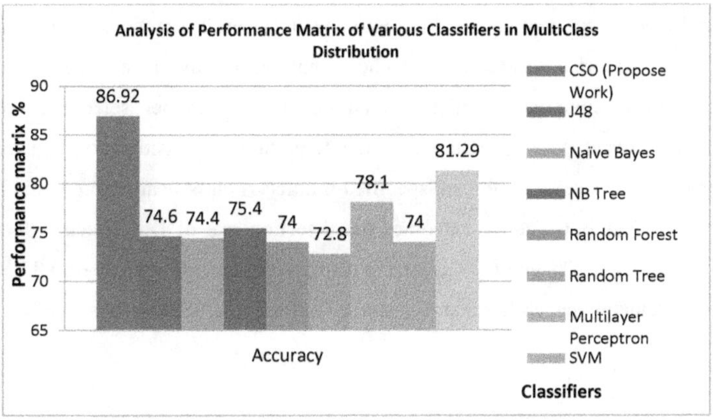

Figure 4.12: Evaluation of Different Classifiers Performance Matrix in Multiclass Distribution

While assessing the effectiveness of different classifiers in a multi-class distribution, a thorough examination of machine learning techniques for jobs involving numerous groups is required, as seen in Figure 4.12. Support vector machines, NB trees, J48, RNN, random forests, and naïve bayes multilayer perceptron are among the classifiers used in this study. Table 4.5 clearly indicates the proposed RF-CSO is superior to the other previous approaches in terms of accuracy.

Table 4.5: Comparative Accuracy Analysis

S. NO.	Algorithm	Accuracy (%)
1.	CNN-GRU[5]	85.05%
2.	CSAGC-IDS [6]	84.55%
3.	Naïve Bayes[7]	85%
4.	J48[8]	79.1%
5.	RF-CSO (Proposed work)	88.48%

4.10 Summary

The classifiers usefulness is assessed using performance measures for each category. Several metrics are evaluated, taking into account overall accuracy, recall and precision for particular categories, to ascertain whichever approach is the most effective at categorizing. Other crucial components of this method, such as model selection, cross-validation techniques, hyper parameter tuning, and interpretability considerations, guarantee that the optimal model is selected for the specified multiclass classification problem. The suggested model provides outstanding outcomes the detection rate of Dos attack is 99.9%, Probe is 97.8%, R2L is 99.7% and U2R is 97.1% respectively and a low FAR of 0.85, demonstrating superior detection capability and robustness with minimal false alarms.

CHAPTER - 5

HYBRID INTRUSION DETECTION SYSTEM USING ANT COLONY AND ARTIFICIAL NEURAL NETWORK

In this chapter a hybrid combination of ANN and ACO techniques is used to develop IDS framework. First, the NSL_KDD dataset is cleaned up to remove redundant information and distortion. After clustering, the best characteristics are selected using the Ant Colony Optimization (ACO) method. ACO mimics how ants hunt for food to identify the most crucial components for categorization problems. The system's performance is evaluated using metrics like false alarm rate, accuracy, and detection rate. In comparison to the traditional methods, the proposed ANN-ACO hybrid exhibits an outstanding accuracy of 99%. The system is more dependable since the false alert rate is much decreased. By guaranteeing improved feature representation and lowering computational complexity, the suggested model's accuracy is 99.0%, and its FAR is 0.21 which is better than the previous models. The method exhibits its promise as a reliable and effective way to find network security breaches.

5.1 Introduction

In the previous chapter we have used a hybrid approaches based on Random forest algorithm and crow search algorithm. In order to strengthen the systems and networks against a continuously changing environment, security measures must likewise evolve together with technology. Despite being essential components of computer safety, antivirus programs and firewalls are not completely impenetrable, leaving systems vulnerable to sophisticated assaults. IDS are designed especially to examine network traffic for oddities or trends that could indicate malicious activity. Extensive learning enhances these systems effectiveness, which is essential for distinguishing among safe user conduct and possible dangers. In this chapter we proposed hybrid intrusion detection system using ant colony and artificial neural network because ACO efficiently performs feature selection and parameter optimization, reducing redundant and irrelevant network features, while ANN excels at learning complex, non-linear attack patterns from data. By combining ACO with ANN, the system achieves improved detection accuracy.

5.2 Proposed Artificial Neural Network and Ant Colony Optimization

Framework of the proposed approach based on ANN and ACO is shown in Figure 5.3, the processing start with the feature selection of then applies the ANN to divide the dataset into six clusters and then uses the Ant colony optimization technique identify the normal and attack instances.

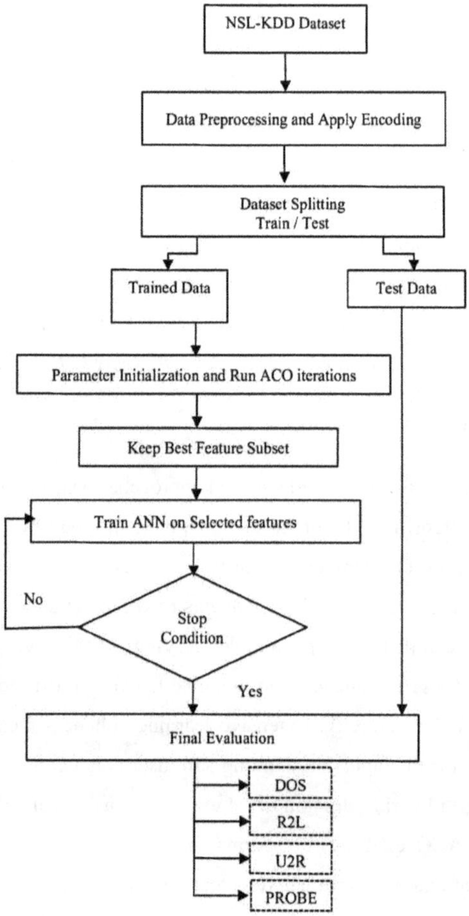

Figure 5.1: Proposed ANN and ACO Framework

5.3 K-RMS Clustering Technique

The basis of the K-RMS algorithm is the technique for clustering known as the K-Means algorithm. It iteratively improves clustering accuracy, starting with k starting cluster centers. First, each point's smallest distance from the centroid determines which cluster it belongs to. Nevertheless, it has serious limitations, including a high number of cycles and lower accuracy for signed data. This is because the centroid of the cluster is found using the average value in the K-Means approach [99].

The technique known as K-Means has been changed to modify the way clustering is achieved by allocating the centroid to counteract this. RMS can deal with "contradictory" data elements more effectively and minimize repetitions since it places greater emphasis on bigger variances over basic average. For large datasets, it is anticipated that the number of iterations will be significantly decreased when the RMS (Root Mean Square) values is used instead of the average value. This is because RMS values are much more accurate and converge more quickly across all scientific fields. Datasets with negative values are also managed. The algorithm's process undergoes a significant reduction in the quantity of change that takes place when the average value is used [100].

Step 1: Assuming *m* data points and the dataset's feature 1 is indicated as

$$A = \{\alpha_1, \alpha_2, \alpha_3, \ldots\ldots \alpha_m\}$$

The second feature in the dataset is marked by set

$$B = \{\beta_1, \beta_2, \beta_3, \ldots\ldots \beta_m\}$$

To begin, it generates an arbitrary number of centroids whose count matches the total quantity of clusters where the data will be separated. In this case, C stands for the centroids, and N is the quantity of clusters.

$$C= \{(\alpha_1, \beta_1), (\alpha_2, \beta_2), \ldots(\alpha_N, \beta_N)\}$$

These centroids initial values are determined at random. If a point (x, y) is to be allocated to any of the center points, a mean Euclidean distance across each of the data points is obtained individually from every centroid, and the distance is denoted by D.

Consider a centroid (α_j, β_j) and a point (α_i, β_i) where $1 \leq j \leq M$ and $1 \leq i \leq n$ and currently the Euclidean distance between (α_i, β_i) and (α_j, β_j) is represent d as D_{ij}.

$$D_{ij} = \sqrt{((\alpha i - \alpha j)^2 + (\beta i - \beta j)^2)}$$

In order to bring the length determined by geometry of Euclid closer to the threshold of the converging particular, it is modified based on the quantity of data elements. It has been discovered that it reduces the number of repetitions while being accurate. For each (N_i), (D_{ij}) produces the centroid (N_j, M_j) for which the data point is assigned. The same technique is repeated for the remaining centroids and data points.

Step 2: The RMS (Root Mean Square) measure of every point designated to a centroid is derived for both the Y and X coordinate positions of all these points and the recently produced value (αRMS, βRMS) is chosen as the currently selected centroid as

$$\alpha RMS = J\_(((\alpha\_1^{\wedge}2+\alpha\_2^{\wedge}2+\cdots+\alpha\_n^{\wedge}2\ )/n)) \quad (5.1)$$

$$\beta RMS = J\_(((\beta\_1^{\wedge}2+\beta\_2^{\wedge}2+\cdots+\beta\_n^{\wedge}2\ )/n))\ )) \quad (5.2)$$

This technique is performed for each centroid that has been initialized.

Step 3: Measure the distance between each centroid's beginning and end positions. The term "shift" refers to this distance. A shifting threshold has already been established. If the shift is less than the set threshold, no more iteration is done for that centroid.

Step 4: When a new set of centroids has been created, redo step-1; here, the span between every site is calculated and assigned appropriately. The highest and lowest deviations were additionally determined, which are just the minimum and maximum intervals between the data point and the centroid after a specific number of iterations of the median squared distance.

5.4 Artificial Neural Network

A network of linked basic units called neurons makes up an Artificial Neural Network (ANN). A standard ANN is made up of three sections: output, hidden, and input. Input feature vectors are distributed to the neuroses in the input layer. The weights of neurons connections have been boosted by the information obtained by each neuron in the output and hidden layers. The neurons subsequently generate output through combining the information and sending it via a transfer mechanism [79].

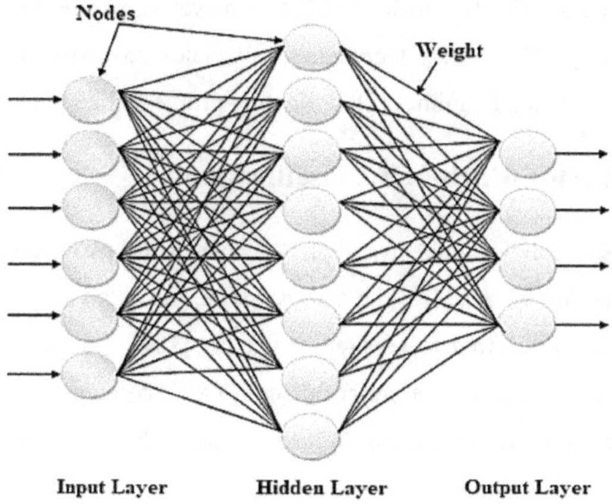

Figure 5.2: ANN's Structure

The ANN's input layer is described below:

$$\{i_1, d_1\}, \{i_2, d_2\}, \cdots, \{i_q, d_q\}$$

Where i_q represents the network's input and d_q identifies the associated goal. The network is trained iteratively. The MSE is calculated by comparing the aim with the system output at each cycle. Here's how the MSE statistic is calculated:

$$F(X) = (t_k - x_k)^2 \quad (5.3)$$

Here, (X) represents the MSE function, whereas x_k and t_k represent the yield and objective of the kth iteration, correspondingly. Back Propagation (BP) is a popular technique for training ANNs utilizing the Levenberg-Marquardt approach. The BP is a method for minimizing the projected MSE by altering the significance of the linking weights. The successive weight alteration technique is usually used once the error function's minimum is achieved or the MSE achieves a low level sufficient to accurately recognize the input variables. The masses inside the nth layer are determined by, in the $(k + 1)^{th}$ iteration.

$$v_{ij}^{n}(k+1) = v_{ij}^{n}(k) - A\frac{\partial F(x)}{\partial v_{jj}^{n}} \tag{5.4}$$

Because BP is a fast, effective technique that achieves convergence quickly. Additionally, like several other gradient query techniques, BP yields inconsistent and surprising results when used to sophisticated nonlinear classification problems like ANNs.

5.5 Support Vector Machine's Classification

The SVM seeks out the optimal hyper plane between the two classes and positions it to maximize the margin. To establish the starting point, the data values that are closest to that separating border are referred to as support vectors [101]. Consider that within a specific training set $G = \{x_i, y_i\}$, there is a preferred significance belonging to the class described by $\in\{+1,-1\}$for each input vector $x_i \in Rd$. Figure 5.5 shows the SVM Classification.

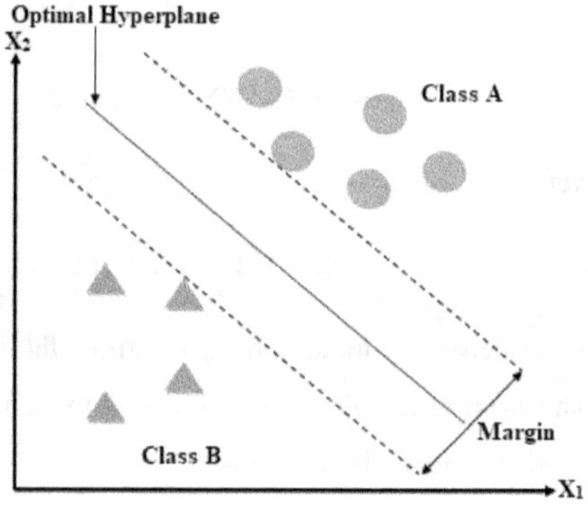

Figure 5.5: SVM Classifications [102]

The class to which the position x_i belongs is indicated by, which is either +1 or 1. The x_i is a legitimate value in d-dimensional vector. The identification mechanism of the form is created using margin. Support Vector Machines may be thought of as a delicate balance among accuracy and adaptability, whereas the model creates a rule of distinction which keeps robustness over ambiguity in unknown cases rather than just trying to match limits to facts.

The support vector machine finds the optimal hyper plane between two distinct groups in order to optimize variance. The data values that are closest to the margin-defining separating boundary are known as support vectors. Within a particular training set $S = \{X_i, Y_j\}$, each input vector $X_i \in Rd$ has a preferred significance that belongs to the class denoted by $X \in \{+1, -1\}$. Position X_i belongs to a class denoted by Y_i, which is either +1 or −1. A valid value in a d-dimensional vector is x_i. Support vector machine is used to generate the form's identifying mechanism.

$$F(X) = (v, \Phi(X)) + y, \ \Phi: U^d \rightarrow T, v \in T \quad (5.5)$$

The coefficients are represented by $\{v_i\}_{i=1}^{m}$, whereas the data in feature space is represented by $\{\Phi\ (x_i)\}_{i=1}^{m}$. By minimizing the risk function provided below, these are computed.

$$U(G) = G \frac{1}{W} \Sigma_{i=1}^{m} T_e(Y_i, f(X)) + ½|v|^2 \quad (5.6)$$

where G is the constant value and $T_e(Y_i, f(X))$ represents the weight vector needed to calculate the approximated deviations between the computed and predicted outputs. There is ½|v|2 determines the trade-off between prediction performance and generalization performance. An approximation of the flatness of the function is given by the second term. The limited function below is the result of adding the relaxation factor, ζ^*, ζ.

$$minimize\ I = ½|v|^2 + G\ \Sigma_{i=1}^{m}(\zeta_i^* + \zeta) \quad (5.7)$$

Subject to (ζ_i^*, ζ), $(Y_i - [v, \Phi(X)] - y <= \epsilon + \zeta_i^*)$, $[[v, \Phi(X)] + y <= \epsilon + \zeta_i^*)$

Lastly, by applying the optimum constraints and adding Lagrange multipliers, it is expressed explicitly,

$$f(X) = \Sigma_{i=1}^{m}(A_i . A_i^*)S(X_i - X) + y \quad (5.8)$$

For i representing the integer values that connect 1 and M, the Lagrange multiplication coefficients A_i and A_i^* satisfy the equality conditions $A_i^* \geq 0$, $A_i^* \times A_i = 0$, and $A_i \geq 0$. To find the multiplying factors of Lagrange A_i* and A_i, reduce to the subsequent form.

$$\text{Min}J\ I = \frac{1}{2}\Sigma_{i=1}^{m}(A_i - A_i^*)(A_i^* - A_i)S(X_i, X_k) + \Sigma_{i=1}^{m}(A_i^*(Y_i - €) + \Sigma_{i=1}^{m}(A_i^*(Y_i + €)$$

$$\text{Subject to } \Sigma_{i=1}^{m}A_i = \Sigma_{i=1}^{m} A_i^*, 0 <= A_i^* <= G, 0 <= A_i <= G$$

5.6.1 Ant Colony Optimization

The dataset created by the NSL_KDD is frequently employed for networked attack identification approach formation and assessment. When employed in network infrastructures, the dataset simulates both regular and malicious traffic, allowing researchers to create and evaluate IDS systems within specified circumstances [97]. For training hybrid systems and machine learning models, it is very helpful. Such as combinations of clustering and classification algorithms. By preprocessing the dataset removing noise and irrelevant features an IDS can identify key characteristics of normal and malicious behavior [96].

When deployed in a network scenario, the IDS trained on NSL_KDD data analyzes incoming traffic and flags suspicious activities based on patterns it has learned. This helps in detecting anomalies, minimizing false positives, and reducing response times. NSL_KDD balanced design makes it possible to measure performance more accurately, which makes it a useful tool for creating adaptable, dependable systems. Because of its comprehension, affordability, and solid basis for evaluating a broad range of ML, DL, and hybrid safety techniques, NSL_KDD is still often used in academics as a standard. It still acts as a vital first step for scientists creating more sophisticated and reliable intrusion detection technologies.

5.6 Results and Discussion

Hybrid classifiers ANN and ACO are used to analyze cluster-based IDS. The NSL_KDD dataset is used to evaluate the proposed method, and Python is used for executing the results. A cluster-based intrusion detection system's effectiveness is assessed using a range of parameters.

5.6.1 Evaluation Matrices

A variety of matrices are used to evaluate the suggested method's performance. In Table 5.2, the confusion matrix is displayed.

Table 5.1: Confusion Matrix

	Classification	
	Attack	Normal
Attack	TN	FN
Normal	FP	TP

Here FN denotes incidences that were wrongly forecasted as non-attacks, TP indicates occurrences that had been successfully expected as non-attacks, TP indicates occurrence that was appropriately predicted as assaults, and FP indicates instances that were erroneously expected as attacks. The proposed parameters are mathematically expressed as follows:

$$\text{Detection Rate} = TP/TP + FN \quad (5.9)$$

$$\text{False Alarm Rate} = FP/FP + TN \quad (5.10)$$

The other parameters are mention in the previous chapter from equation 4.6 to equation 4.10.

5.6.2 Comparative Analysis

The new hybrid classifier technique and the old approaches are first compared in terms of accuracy across all clustered data. Table 5.3 depicts the accuracy analysis for NSL_KDD dataset. The proposed hybrid ANN-SVM method has 5.4%, 8.0% and 1.6 % higher accuracy for KNN, Fuzzy and FNN method.

Table 5.2: Accuracy Comparison

Method	**Accuracy**
KNN	93.6%
Fuzzy	91%
FNN	97.4%
GRU	97.1%
Multilayered	98.1%
ANN-ACO (Proposed Method)	99.0%

A visual bar chart is used to illustrate the accuracy of the suggested methodology, making it simple to see how much better it performs than the current intrusion detection system. As a result, Figure 5.6 displays a visual bar chart showing accuracy based on both the suggested and current methods. This formula can be used to calculate the intrusion detection accuracy. The suggested method's total accuracy is 99%; compared to existing methods like KNN, SVM, and ANN.

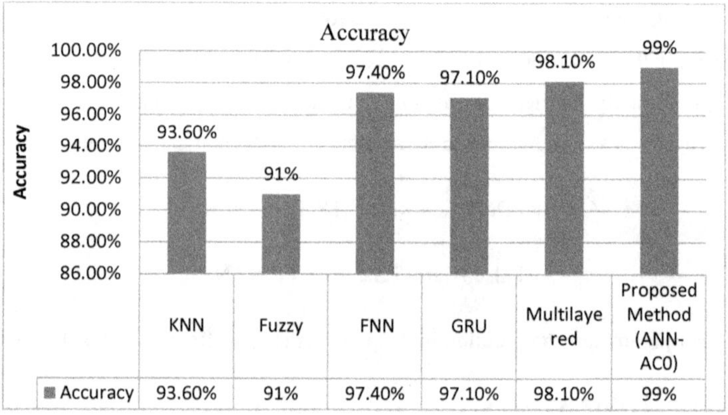

Figure 5.4: Assessment of Accuracy

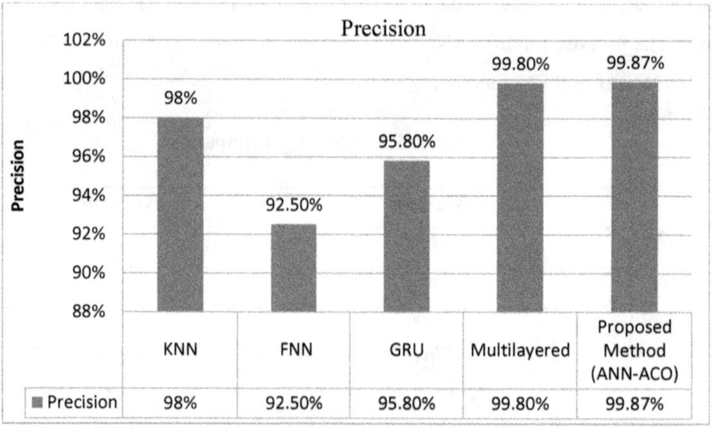

Figure 5.5: Precision Rate Assessments

In this the percentage precision rate for the current KNN, FNN, and GRU system is 98.00%, 92.50%, and 95.80%, respectively. This is lower than the suggested approach's detection rate of 99.87%, demonstrating the superior performance of the suggested hybrid classifier. The high-performance suggested system's graphical chart of precision is shown in Figure 5.7.

The suggested strategy performs significantly better than the proposed ways when compared to several existing strategies for attacking detection. The frequency of false alarms is shown graphically below. The IDS false alert rate is then examined for both the suggested and current approaches. The false alarm rate figures are tabulated.

Table 5.3: False Alarm Rate Comparison

Method	FAR
KNN	0.69
Fuzzy	0.62
FNN	0.53
GRU	0.41
Multilayered	0.59
ANN-ACO (Proposed Method)	0.21

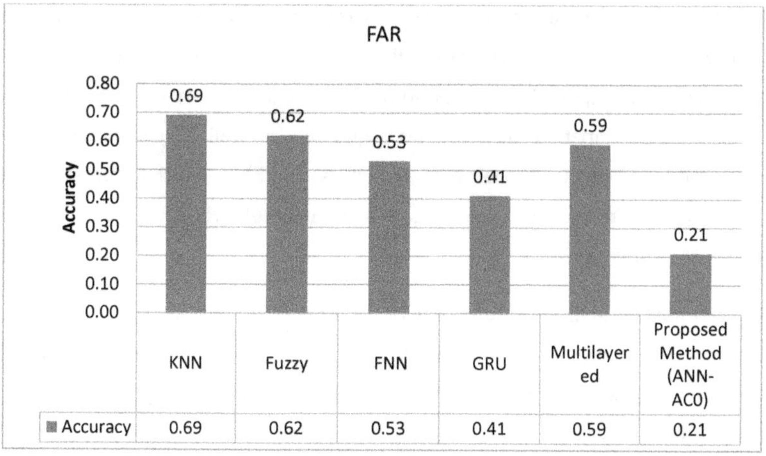

Figure 5.6: Comparative Analysis of False Alarm Rate

The various false alarm rates for the various algorithmic techniques are shown in Table 5.4. The findings demonstrate that, in comparison to the other approaches currently in use, the FAR rate value is lower for all previous methods. Figure 5.8 is an illustration of a false alert rate in relation to the existing and recommended methods. Interference, noise, and cluster detection are its primary applications.

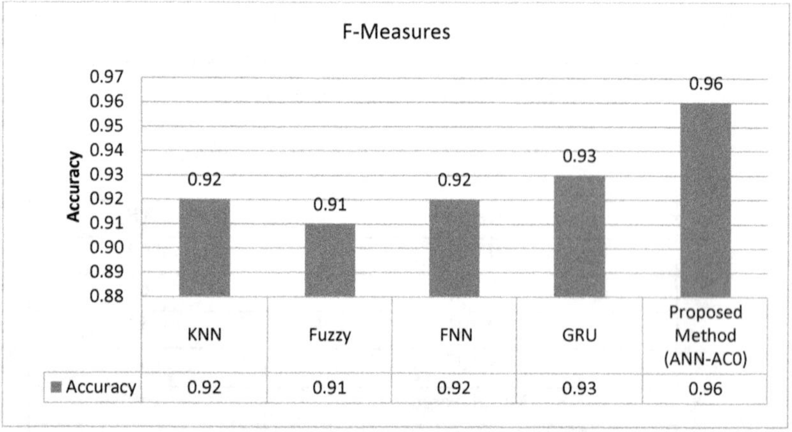

Figure 5.7: Comparative Analysis of F-measure

Similarly, the suggested system's F-Measure is greater compared to any of the current K-NN, GRU, and FNN systems. In contrast to the suggested model, which has a high value of 0.96, As a result, the suggested method performs better than the current models. Figure 5.9 shows the F-Measure variations between the suggested as well as current approaches. When compared to the existing models of KNN, Fuzzy, and FNN, which have F-Measures of 0.92, 0.91, and 0.92, respectively, the suggested approach of hybrid classifier SVM-ANN has a high F-Measure of 0.96

The comparative analysis of recall rate of the proposed hybrid ANN-ACO model is shown in Figure 5.10. The suggested approach executes better than the previous techniques makes the advantages of the suggested structure clear. The suggested strategy performs better than the existing method when examined side by side the recall rate effectiveness for the proposed and prior methods is analyzed across the NSL_KDD dataset.

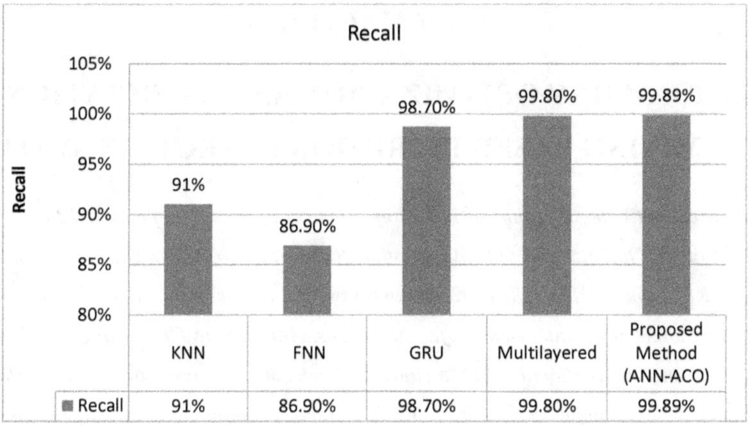

Figure 5.8: Comparative Analysis of Recall Rate

5.7 Summary

The combined classifications linked to the ANN and ACO algorithms two essential methods for intrusion detection have been identified by researchers who are interested in solving classification problems. Clustering-based categorization was used in this work to find intrusions. To start, the NSL_KDD data are pre-processed to eliminate extraneous noise. After this is finished, The ANN method is used for clustering the data. According to data efficiency, this algorithm groups all of the data into the relevant cluster groupings. The best characteristics are then chosen by using the ACO. After that, the process of classification decides if the data points to malicious or typical behavior. A hybrid classification approach for data forecasting is suggested, using both ANN and ACO. The NSL_KDD dataset's performance was assessed through trials. Excellent precision and recognition rates are revealed by the study's findings.

CHAPTER - 6

ANT COLONY OPTIMIZATION AND ASSOCIATION RULE MINING BASED INTRUSION DETECTION SYSTEM

For excellent categorization of intrusion a hybrid approach is proposed that combine the Ant Colony Optimization with Association Rule Mining (ARM). The system processes the NSL_KDD and KDD CICIoT2023 datasets by first removing noise and then using ARM to cluster connections into meaningful subgroups. Ant Colony Optimization (ACO) takes the role of the conventional PSO method for selecting features to improve classification efficiency. ACO improves accuracy while lowering computing overhead by simulating ant behavior to find the most pertinent information. In terms of false alarm rate, detection rate, and computational speed, the hybrid ACO+ARM classifier outperforms conventional classifiers such as KNN, standalone SVM, and ANN by utilizing these features. For certain clusters, testing on the NSL_KDD dataset showed a rate of false alarms as low as 0.07 and a detection accuracy of 98.80%; the CICIoT2023 dataset produced even better results. For network security and real-time cloud applications, the IDS are scalable and extremely effective at detecting intrusions. The system provides strong, dependable, and scalable solutions to network intrusion detection problems by using clustering and hybrid classification's advantages and combining ACO for optimal feature selection.

6.1 Introduction

In this chapter, clustering-based intrusion detection is executed to the NSL_KDD collection. The selected data is clustered using the ARM technique. After cluster completion, the hybrid classifiers which are carried out by the ACO and ARM algorithms are used to identify both normal and malicious activity. This chapter explains the details on the ARM clustering technique, the ACO+ARM algorithm, and the overall design.

6.1.1 Dataset Description

Having a sufficient dataset is essential for any comparative study on cloud incursion. Attack identification uses the NSL_KDD collection to distinguish between normal and malicious activity [103]. In the KDD Archive, the NSL_KDD dataset is the most significant Network Intrusion Evaluation dataset. Each of the 41 attributes in the dataset is represented as a separate connection vector [104]. The vectors are categorized as Attack or Normal. 10% of the dataset may be accessed online and used as a training set; this includes about five lac instances [109]. In the training set, normal connections make up 19.69% of the connections, whereas attack connections make up 80.31%.

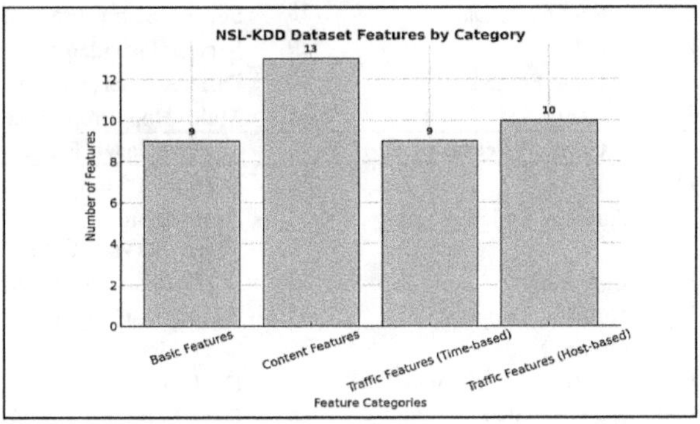

Figure 6.1: Distribution of different Types of Attacks in NSL_KDD Dataset

Figure 6.1 depicts the categorization of the NSL_KDD data features, which include 4 types of features. Table 6.1 depicts the many assault categories divided into four primary categories [105].

Table 6.1: Attacks Classes

Types	Attack category							
U2R	Buffer Overflow	Http tuneel	Rootkit	LoadModule	Perl	Xtern, Ps	SQL attacks	-
R2L	WarezMaster	Imap	Spy	Sendmail	Xsnoop	Multihop	Phf	Guess Password,
DOS	Apache2	Neptune	Pod	Land	Smurf	Mailbomb	-	-
PROBE	Satan	Saint	Ipsweep	Portsweep	Nmap	Mscan	-	-

Table 6.2: Features of Dataset [110]

List of NSL –KDD features			
	Basic Features		**Traffic Features**
1	Time Limit	23	Counter_0
2	Form Of Protocol	24	Link_Counter
3	Service	25	Error_Proportion
4	Flag	26	Ervice_Error_Log
5	Source Node Data	27	Rejection_Error_Log
6	Target Node Data	28	Service_Error_Proportion
7	Land	29	Service Provider_Proportion
8	Wrong_Fragment	30	Different_Service_Proportion
9	Urgent	31	Multi_Hop_Proportion
	Content Feature		**Host Based Feature**
11	Hot	32	Destitaion_Hop_Counter
12	Attempt_Failed_Logins	33	Destination _Host_Service_Counter
13	Log_Innput	34	D _H_Identical_ Service_Rate
14	Number_Cooperated	35	D _ Multi-Hop_Service_Rate
15	Origin_Node	36	D_H_Identical_Source Port
16	Su_Root_Endeavored	37	D_H_ Service_Multi-Host
17	Root_Number	38	D_H_Service_Error_Rate
18	File_Creation_Log	39	D_H_Service_Error_Rate
19	Itration_Shells_Log	40	D_H_Req_Error_Rate
20	Access_Files_Itration	41	D_H_ Service_Req_Error_Rate
21	Outbound_Cmds_Itration		
22	Is_Threat_Login		D-Destination,
23	Is_Visitor Node_Login		H-Host

The four distinct characteristics of the NSL collection are illustrate in Table 6.2, with 41 attributes falling into the categories of basic, traffic, content, or host-based characteristics. These aspects are crucial to the data's categorization. [106][120].

6.2 Proposed Ant Colony Optimization with Association Rule Mining

Clustering-based categorization is used to find the incursion. The first step is pre-processing the data to eliminate extraneous noise. The ARM algorithm is used to make clusters of pre-processed data. The best characteristics are chosen using the ACO technique. The data of typical or malicious activity is then predicted using the categorization method. The goal of the lone predictor is to attain high accuracy and detection rates. ARM and ACO are examples of hybrid classifiers that are used to identify destructive or normal behavior. The categorization of attack and non-attack data shows the influence of the suggested classifier's effectiveness when compared to traditional algorithms for the insight discovery dataset's.

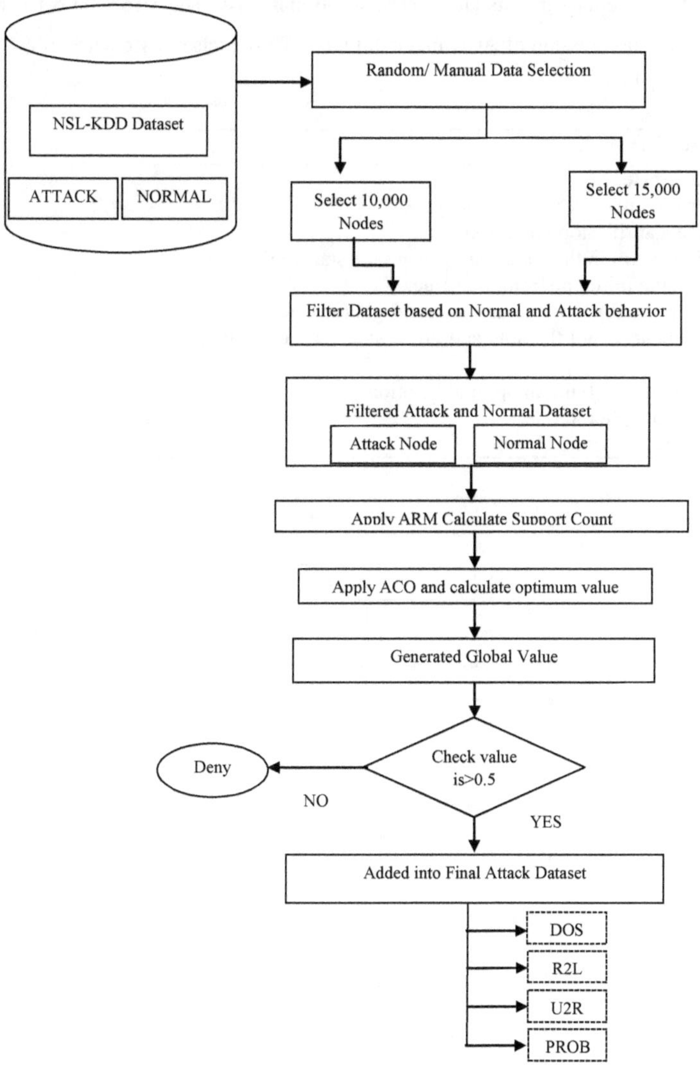

Figure 6.2: Proposed ARM+ACO

Figure 6.2 display the flow of proposed work; here we take a sample of 10,000 and 15,000 node out of overall dataset then pre-process it after that the apply the ARM algorithm in this on the basis on matching factor we divide the data into six subcategories then apply the ACO algorithm to filter the data into its attack class or normal class. The algorithm 6.1 displays the step wise step progression of ACO method. Figure 6.3 depicts the sequence of activities using the ACO methodologies.

Algorithm 6.1: ACO

Step 1: Instigate.
Step 2: Initiation of Parameter for ant.
Step 3: Repeat till Stop condition.
Step 4: Place Ant in the start and evaluate the start region.
Step 5: Set the initial pheromone value.
Step 6: Explore for food and update local pheromone.
Step 7: Repeat for all the ants and go-to step 2 if stop condition not satisfy.
Step 8: stop if ants built an optimal solution.
Step 9: Update pheromone.
Step 10: End iteration.

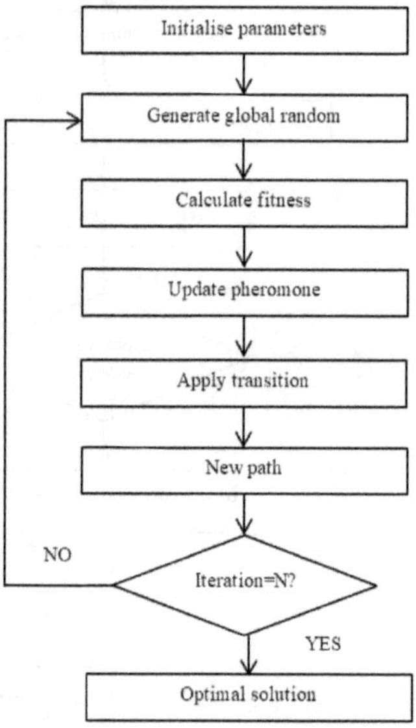

Figure 6.3: Flow Chart of ACO Algorithm

Algorithm 6.2: The ARM+ACO

1: Input: ID (icv1, icv2, icv3……icvn)
2: Output: OD (odv1, odv2, odv3…..odvn)
3: Terminology:
ID->Input Dataset, CV->Column Value, OD->Output Data, ODV->Output Data Value, n->Nodes, AN->Attack Nodes, SPP->Start Pheromone Path,
PP->Pheromone Path, EV->Evaporation Value, ADS->Attack Data Set
SV->Support Value.
5: Step 1: Select IDS (icv1, icv2, icv3……icvn)
6: Step 2: Filter input dataset based on the feature 4 and feature 6 values.
7: Step3: Again filter nodes based on successfully send and received values.
8: Step 4: Now take Probable unfiltered node to calculate Support on the basis of matching factors shown in Table 17, Table 18 and Table 19.
9: Step 5: Create support table having six SV (SV1, SV2…… SV6) on dataset feature.
10: Step 6: Support->Outcome of ID1/Total Probability in ID.
11: Step 7: Take Threshold value as 0.5
12: Step 8:
13: a.) Take Value of SV1, SV2…… SV6
14: b.) Iteration j=1 to 3 do
15: SPP= (∑SV1+SV2….SV6)/6
16: If (SPP>=0.5)
17: Osv1=PP1, Osv2=PP2………..OSVn=PPn
18: For 2 to 3 do
19: PP=SPP+ (∑SV1+SV2….SV6)/6-EV
20: EV={0.2,0.4}
21: If(j=1)
22: SPP1=SPP
23: If(j=2)
24: SPP2=SSP1+SSP-EV (0.2)
25: If(j=3)
26: SPP3=SSP2+SSP-EV(0.4)
27: Step 9: if(SSP3>0.5)
28: ADS= {odv1, odv2, odv3…..odvn}
29: Step10: Repeat step 5 to step 9 on all nodes for detection of normal or attack node.
30: Step11: Final ADS will accomplish.
31: Step12: add ADS in filtered attack nodes and form an absolute attack Dataset.

The algorithm 6.2 shows step wise step progression on the attack and normal node classification.

6.2.1 Data Selection

The proposed approaches for intrusion detection of clustered data are examined using NSL_KDD collection [111]. To verify the framework out of complete dataset 10,000 and 15,000 nodes are selected in the random manner, Figure 6.4 and Figure 6.5 displays the numbers of nodes belong to a particular attack categories and the selection of the record is done on the basis of the percentages of the data available in the actual dataset out of 125,973 nodes [112][113].

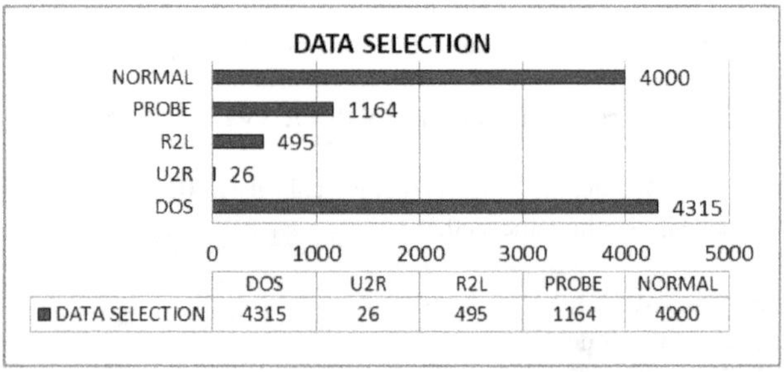

Figure 6.4: Selections of Data (10,000)

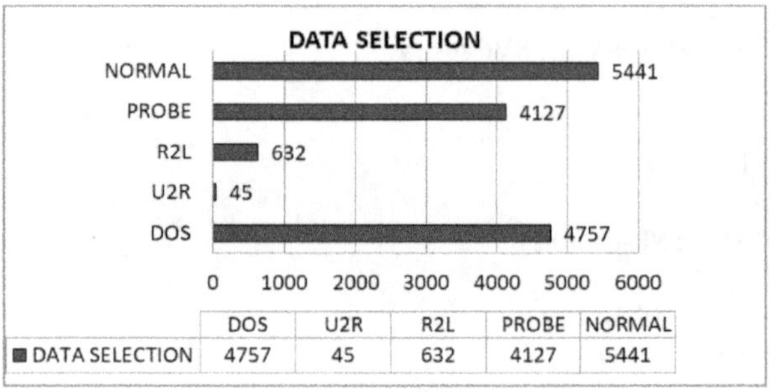

Figure 6.5: Selections of Data (15,000)

6.2.2 Performance Assessment

In relation to the NSL_KDD the datasets, both accuracy and the detection frequency, computing complexities, and false alarm rate efficiency features are evaluated and analyzed for the proposed arrangement [107][108].

6.2.3 Simulation Results

The Algorithm 6.1 (ACO) and Algorithm 6.2 (ARM+ACO) display the flow of work. The outlined method's efficiency is assessed using the NSL_KDD dataset. After removing duplicate records, we use ARM to group the data set into six categories based on the dataset attributes listed in Table 6.3, Table 6.4, and Table 6.5, respectively. These clusters are processed by the ACO technique using a threshold limit 0.5 the result shows the improvement of the proposed work as compared to the previous methodology in all the calculated parameters.

Table 6.3: Content Features (10-22) [114][115][116]

0	0	0	0	0	0	0	0	0	0	0	0	0
0	0	1	0	0	0	0	0	0	0	0	0	0

Table 6.4: Traffic Features (23-31)

136	1	0.00	0.00	1.00	1.000	0.01	0.06	0.00
33	47	0.00	0.00	0.00	0.000	1.00	0.00	0.4

Table 6.5: Host –Based Features (32-41)

255	1	0.00	0.06	0.00	0.00	0.00	0.00	1.00	1.00
151	255	1.00	0.00	0.01	0.03	0.00	0.00	0.00	0.00

The accuracy comparisons of the four kinds of attacks and typical cases are shown in Figure 6.6. The suggested system's efficacy is thoroughly evaluated. Its effectiveness is directly contrasted with a variety of well-known ML techniques. The area of security surveillance frequently uses such standard techniques. The method developed has a definite benefit, according to the comparison study. In particular, the outcomes of the hybrid relationship between ARM and ACO continuously demonstrate its outstanding characteristics. This novel interaction paradigm turns out to be quite advantageous. The fundamental components that characterize the success of the ARM+ACO paradigm are methodically introduced.

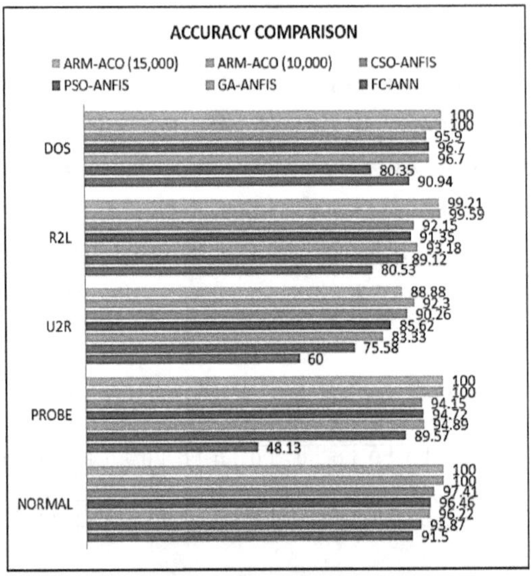

Figure 6.6: Accuracy Comparison

Table 6.6 goes into great depth about these vital aspects, which are necessary to comprehend how it works and what effects it has. This table offers a detailed look at the elements influencing the increased efficiency of the ARM+ACO system. Considering these variables is crucial to grasping how our hybrid algorithm improves typical ML approaches in IDS systems.

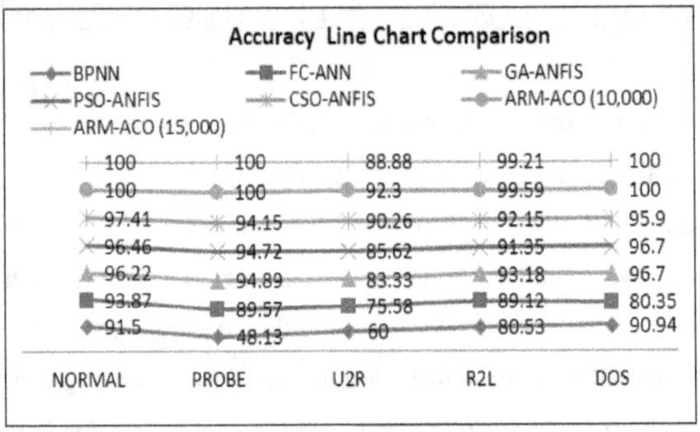

Figure 6.7: Comparative Analysis of Accuracy

Figure 6.7 clearly display the improvement of the proposed system over pervious methodology and accuracy of the system is much promising in all most all types of attack detection. The suggested technique outperforms the previous, as evidenced by its increased accuracy.

Table 6.6: ARM+ACO Model Parameters

Specification	ARM-ACO
Type	Sugeno
Input/output	4/1
No. of MFs for each input	7
No. of output MFs	7
Input MF	Gaussian
Output MF	Linear
No. of Arm rule	6
No. of Non-linear parameters	112
No. of linear parameters	30
No. of ants for each population	40

Table 6.7: FAR Comparison

Techniques	FAR (%)
BP-NN	6.10
FC-ANN	4.37
GA-ANFIS	3.75
PSO-ANFIS	3.38
CSO-ANFIS	3.45
ARM-ACO (Proposed work) NSL_KDD	0.035
ARM-ACO (Proposed work) CICIoT2023	0.07

Intrusion detection FAR for both the suggested and current approaches is then computed and tabulated. The Table 6.7 represents comparison between the FAR. The proposed ARM+ACO having 0.07 FAR in CICIoT2023 dataset and 0.035 FAR in the NSL_KDD dataset respectively this clearly shows that the proposed work is far better as compared to the previous models.

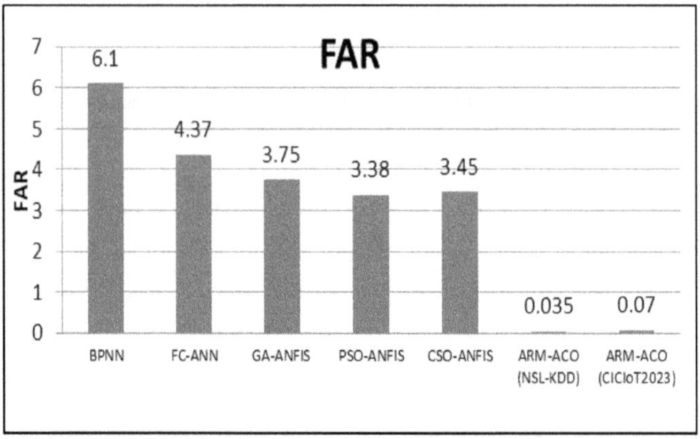

Figure 6.8: FAR Comparison

The hybrid classifier's false alarm rate is shown in Figure 6.8. The suggested ARM+ACO approach has a false alarm rate is 0.035 in NSL_KDD dataset, which is less than the false alarm rates of the other previous approaches.

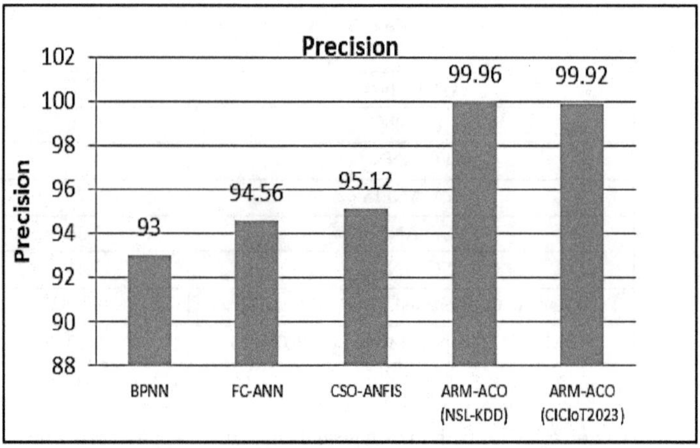

Figure 6.9: Precision Comparison

The hybrid classifier's precision is shown in Figure 6.9. The result indicates that the precision rate is superior to the recent hybrid models. The ARM+ACO have 99.96%

precision in NSL_KDD dataset and 99.92% in the CICIoT2023 dataset. The implemented hybrid ARM+ACO framework is also tested against the recent IoT generated dataset i.e. CICIoT2023 dataset. This new dataset contain 33 categories of attacks including the normal instances having 47 features which contain approx. 232,885 records [118][119]. The proposed system is also tested on the recent dataset known as CICIoT2023 dataset [77][78]. As seen in Figure 6.10, the dataset initially breaks down into training and testing samples. The ARM-ARO technique is then used to this updated data set and the suggested algorithms successful classification rate is 99.93%.

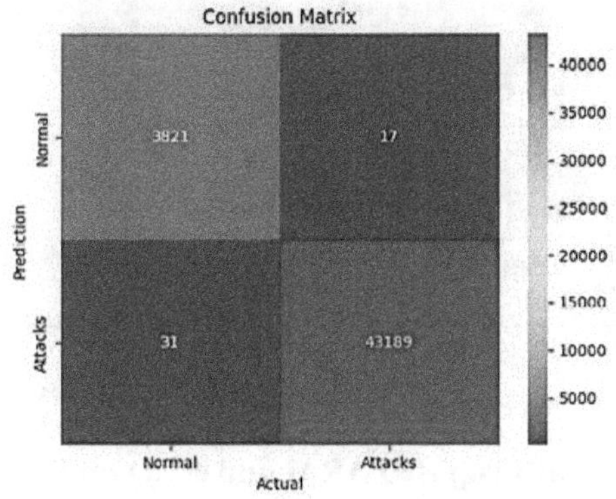

Figure 6.10: CICIoT2023 Binary Classifications

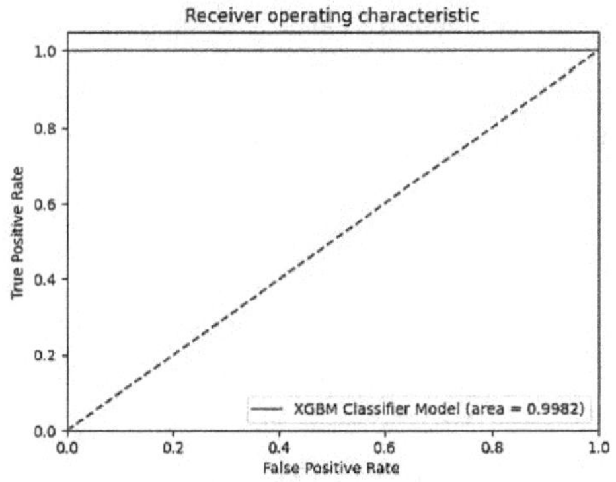

Figure 6.11: CICIoT2023 ROC Curve

To illustrate the greater accuracy of this intrusion detection system approach, Figure 6.12 is present the bar chart of accuracy comparison. The accuracy comparison between the suggested ARM+ACO methods and previous methods respectively. The suggested strategy outperforms the current one in terms of intrusion detection rate, as evidenced by its greater value.

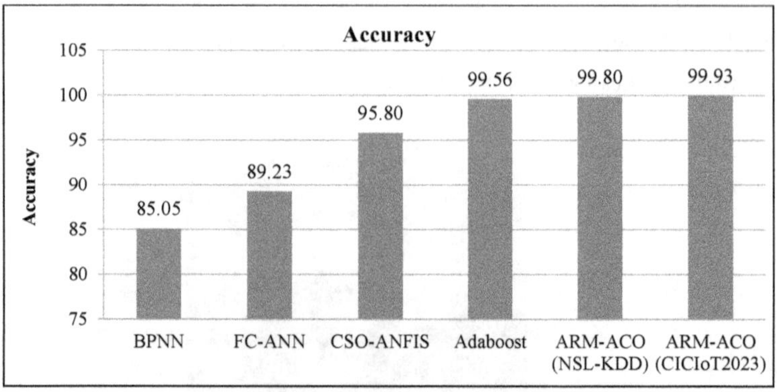

Figure 6.12: Accuracy Comparison

6.3 Comparison of Proposed ARM and ACO on Datasets

The proposed approach ARM and ACO for intrusion detection is examined using the NSL_KDD data set and compared with the previous technique which shows the improved result as compared to the previous technique. Additionally, the proposed technique is also examined on CICIoT2023 clustered data set. The proposed hybrid ARM+ACO algorithm show excellent result in both NSL_KDD as well as in CICIoT2023 dataset which shows the effectiveness of the proposed model.

Table 6.8 presents a comparative analysis of accuracy achieved by various intrusion detection techniques, clearly demonstrating the effectiveness of the proposed ARM and ACO approach. Traditional learning-based methods such as BP-NN and FC-ANN achieve accuracies of 85.05% and 89.23%, respectively, indicating limited detection capability in complex intrusion scenarios. The CSO-ANFIS model shows a notable improvement with an accuracy of 95.80%, reflecting the benefit of optimization-based hybridization. Further enhancement is observed with the CS-RF technique, which achieves an accuracy of 99.00%. In comparison, the proposed ARM-ACO model outperforms all existing approaches, attaining 99.80% accuracy on the NSL-KDD dataset and 99.93% on the CICIoT2023 dataset. This consistent improvement highlights the effectiveness of combining Association Rule Mining with Ant Colony Optimization in reducing misclassification and enhancing overall intrusion detection performance. Moreover, the superior results on the CICIoT2023 dataset demonstrate the adaptability of the proposed model to modern IoT traffic patterns. The findings confirm the scalability and robustness of the ARM-ACO approach for real-world intrusion detection environments.

Table 6.8: Accuracy Evaluation Results

Techniques	Accuracy (%)
BP-NN [1]	85.05
FC-ANN [1]	89.23
CSO-ANFIS [1]	95.80
CS-RF [3]	99.00
ARM-ACO (Proposed work) NSL_KDD	99.80
ARM-ACO (Proposed work) CICIoT2023	99.93

6.4 Summary

Researchers trying to solve classification problems have taken notice of the dual classifications around the ARM and ACO algorithm, which is a significant intrusion detection technique. Clustering-based classification was used in this work to detect the intrusion. To eliminate the undesired noise, the NSL_KDD dataset are first pre-processed. The ARM algorithm is used to make cluster of on pre-processed data. Depending on the data performance, it is used to cluster all the information into the corresponding cluster set. The best characteristics are chosen using the ACO. The classification technique is then used to determine if the data is indicative of normal or malicious activity. To forecast the data, a hybrid classification approach combining ARM and ACO is suggested. Experiments have been conducted to assess the dataset's performance. The findings demonstrate great accuracy and detection rates.

CHAPTER – 7

CONCLUSIONS AND FUTURE ENHANCEMENTS

7.1 CONCLUSIONS

To eliminate extraneous characteristics and distortion within datasets, the current study presents a hybrid approach for intrusion detection that combines a crow search optimization methodology with a neural network-augmented crow search technique is proposed. This method is known as an attributes assessment method. The proposed approach is called hybrid strategy that uses neural networks for both analysis and optimization of crow searches. The performance of these combined techniques is superior to that of any of its individual components. To guarantee the algorithm's accuracy and validity, the suggested algorithm, HCSAOANN, was examined and validated using datasets from the NSL_KDD repository. Several well-known optimization techniques ANN and CSA-CSO are compared to the HCSAOANN algorithm based on certain criteria. Among these are the quantity of selected attributes and the precision of the classifier's output. The recommended HCSAOANN offers the most significant aggregate accuracy in classifying in the available data, as shown by the comparative tests and analyses. Among these are the quantity of selected attributes and the precision of the classifier's output.

In conclusion, the results show the fact that HCSAOANN can outperform other algorithms. Engineering, data science, sentiment analysis, and other fields can all benefit from the HCSAOANN. Enhancing this approach could lead to the implementation of a new selection strategy to identify the least likely characteristics that might be the focus of further study.

The findings demonstrate that, in comparison to alternative approaches, by employing a particular group of the selected attributes, the suggested approach provides the maximum accuracy. This method is seen in other procedures that apply the feature selection strategy to the same dataset. We created a confusion matrix over several attack types regarding attack class and anticipated class to assess the categorization framework's effectiveness across different assault groups both before and after applying the CSO approach. Furthermore, we calculate the Recall and Detection Rate (also called Sensitivity or True Positive Rate), which is essential for assessing a model's classification accuracy both prior to and during CSO The investigation evaluates the effectiveness of the framework parameter for the suggested model and all classes, obtaining outstanding outcomes that include a binary distribution of 88.48% and a multiclass distribution of 86.92%.

This work shows how to use clustering-based classification to detect intrusions in an efficient manner. Prior to clustering using ANN, which groups data into comparable clusters according to performance, the method starts with pretreatment to remove noise. The ACO algorithm is used to choose features optimally, which improves the efficacy of the next classification phase. The system achieves improved prediction capability by using an integrated classification model that combines ANN and ACO, which allows it to differentiate between attacking and normal actions. The suggested method's robustness is confirmed by using the NSL_KDD record to assess the testing procedure, which yielded an astounding 98% accuracy and 97.9% detection rate. This demonstrates its potential to enhance highly accurate and dependable intrusion detection systems.

This work concludes by demonstrating the efficacy of a Using a mixed classifier approaches, finding intrusions by combining ACO with Association Rule Mining (ARM) algorithm. The NSL_KDD dataset is preprocessed to eliminate noise. To improve classification accuracy, the ACO is used to choose the best characteristics. Normal and invasive behaviors are successfully distinguished using the hybrid ACO+ARM classifier. High accuracy and detection rates are demonstrated via experimental assessment, highlighting the approach's potential to overcome classification issues in intrusion detection technologies.

The performance comparison presented in the Table 6.9 highlights the effectiveness of different hybrid intrusion detection approaches in terms of accuracy, precision, and false alarm rate (FAR). The HCSAOANN model presented in chapter 3 achieves an accuracy and precision of 98%, indicating reliable detection capability, though it exhibits a comparatively higher FAR of 0.45. The RF-CSO approach presented in chapter 4 records a moderate accuracy of 88.48% with a precision of 88.5%, reflecting reasonable classification performance but a higher FAR of 0.82, which suggests increased false positives. In contrast, the ANN-ACO model presented in chapter 5 demonstrates significant improvement, achieving 99.00% accuracy and 99% precision with a reduced FAR of 0.21. Further enhancement is observed with the ARM-ACO approach presented in chapter 6 evaluated on the NSL-KDD dataset, attaining 99.80% accuracy and 99.96% precision while maintaining a very low FAR of 0.035. The best performance is achieved by the ARM-ACO model on the CICIoT2023 dataset, which records 99.93% accuracy, 99.92% precision, and an exceptionally low FAR of 0.007, demonstrating superior detection capability and robustness with minimal false alarms.

Table 7.1: Overall Comparison of Proposed Techniques

Proposed Techniques	Accuracy (%)	Precision Rate	FAR
HCSAOANN	98%	98%	0.45
RF-CSO	88.48%	88.5%	0.82
ANN-ACO	99.00%	99.87%	0.21
ARM-ACO NSL_KDD	99.80%	99.96%	0.035
ARM-ACO CICIoT2023	99.93%	99.92%	0.007

7.2 FUTURE ENHANCEMENTS

Applications for the suggested study might be found in many other domains, like technology, sentiment assessment, statistics, etc. It could be feasible to determine the least significant characteristics that could be the subject of next research employing a novel choice strategy by improving this procedure. Future studies could examine practical problems such as sentiment analysis, including the identification of cancer. Future developments might improve ANN-ACO-CSO-based intrusion detection systems ability to detect advanced persistent threats and zero-day vulnerabilities in real time. This hybrid method may be used in cloud settings, IoT networks, smart grids, and industrial control systems where efficient and adaptable detection is needed for large and diverse data streams.

www.ingramcontent.com/pod-product-compliance
Lightning Source LLC
LaVergne TN
LVHW010731061126
851857LV00014B/1432